Praise for *How Witchcraft*

"In *How Witchcraft Saved My Life*, Vincent Higginbotham steers us on a turbulent ride through the wild, often painful, journey of growing up. But Higginbotham isn't just advising us on how to grow up, fit in, and tow the party line. Using the power of deep listening, journaling, meditation, activating clairvoyance, banishing demons, setting boundaries, and the queering of our old-time religion, the author takes fledgling witches under his wing and teaches them how to overcome their fears and grow into their magic. A thrill!"

—Amanda Yates Garcia, author
of *Initiated: Memoir of a Witch*

"A brave, moving account of the power magic can have in healing, transformation, and the realization of our hopes and dreams. Vincent Higginbotham shares not only his personal story in a raw, compelling fashion, but he also offers powerful insights into the Craft across a wide variety of subjects, which includes practical suggestions for how to practice and journal prompts. Often, occult authors offer little information about their personal process and journey. The vulnerability and candor here provides a most welcome change!"

—Durgadas Allon Duriel, author of *The Little Work:
Magic to Transform Your Everyday Life*

"*How Witchcraft Saved My Life* is a rock 'n' roll rollercoaster, an industrial touchstone for witchcraft books in the 2020s. If you enter at your own risk, and open the doors of this cinematic, hardcore, raw, and revealing occult-journey—you'll learn the powerful magickal tools Vincent used to combat and survive the wrath of nature's violent interruptions…"

—Alex Kazemi, author of *Pop Magick*

"Vincent Higginbotham is an excellent teacher, who bravely and generously shares his own personal history including traumatic events in order to demonstrate practical, powerful magickal techniques and tools that are sure to help others. *How Witchcraft Saved My Life* is a fine introduction to witchcraft, what it is and what it isn't, packed full of practical lessons that will be of benefit to all readers, from novices to adepts."

—Judika Illes, author of *Encyclopedia of 5000 Spells*

"*How Witchcraft Saved My Life* is not another book about magic and spells; this is a book about the lessons of human beings in search of discovering their own magic and freedom … Vincent leads you to turn on that magical light in the middle of an erstwhile dark journey to discover the transformative power of magic. In this book, Vincent tells us his turbulent life journey, and how it led him to discover the marvelous and winsome potential to change his life, after reading this book, you will feel forced to discover your own magical potential too."

—Elhoim Leafar, author of *The Magical Art of Crafting Charm Bags and Manifestation Magic*

"This manuscript is an ode to the sharp, broken pieces inside that fear they can never be human enough, let alone witch enough. Vincent courageously shares gut wrenching traumas he has endured, inviting us to witness him at his very psyche. In doing so, he gives us the tools and permission to do the same emotional unpacking in our own lives. The practical exercises in this book are excellent, from thoughtful journal prompts to accessible, actionable ideas. Ultimately the richest treasure of this book lies in the unapologetic space Vincent has carved for the intersection of the very real evils of this world and the transcendent power of witchcraft."

—Meg Rosenbriar, cofounder of Witch With Me and author of
The Healing Power of Witchcraft: A New Witches Guide to Rituals and Spells to Renew Yourself and Your World

How
Witchcraft
Saved My
Life

© Jessica Gentry

About the Author

After a decade living on the streets, Vincent Higginbotham (Southeastern US) went to college at the Art Institute of Philadelphia where he graduated with a degree in industrial design. *How Witchcraft Saved My Life* is his first book. *Vincent* means "to conquer," and that is exactly what he has done his entire life. Currently Vincent lives in the southeastern United States with his husband and their two sons. He is dedicated to working with Hekate and teaching people that they can heal just as he has.

VINCENT HIGGINBOTHAM

HOW
Witchcraft
SAVED MY
Life

Practical Advice for
TRANSFORMATIVE MAGICK

LLEWELLYN PUBLICATIONS
WOODBURY, MINNESOTA

First Edition
First Printing, 2021

Book design by Samantha Peterson
Cover design by Kevin R. Brown

Llewellyn Publications is a registered trademark of Llewellyn Worldwide Ltd.

Library of Congress Cataloging-in-Publication Data
Names: Higginbotham, Vincent, author.
Title: How witchcraft saved my life : practical advice for transformative magick / Vincent Higginbotham.
Description: First edition. | Woodbury, Minnesota : Llewellyn Publications, 2021. | Summary: "Author shares personal stories and advice to help struggling Pagans, seekers, and Witches. Contains journal exercises, practical advice, and resources for professional and spiritual help"—provided by publisher.
Identifiers: LCCN 2021005090 (print) | LCCN 2021005091 (ebook) | ISBN 9780738766638 (paperback) | ISBN 9780738766775 (ebook)
Subjects: LCSH: Witchcraft. | Magic.
Classification: LCC BF1566 .H54 2021 (print) | LCC BF1566 (ebook) | DDC 133.4/3—dc23
LC record available at https://lccn.loc.gov/2021005090
LC ebook record available at https://lccn.loc.gov/2021005091

Llewellyn Publications
A Division of Llewellyn Worldwide Ltd.
2143 Wooddale Drive
Woodbury, MN 55125-2989
www.llewellyn.com

Printed in the United States of America

Contents

Content Warning

This book deals with sensitive topics including molestation, suicide, child abuse, drug abuse, prostitution, conversion therapy, and homelessness. While I have done my best to portray my experiences in a tasteful and respectful manner, these subjects may be troubling for some readers and inappropriate for others. Discretion is advised.

Disclaimer

If you or someone you know is experiencing abuse or any of the situations discussed in this book, please know there is help available. No one should suffer for who they are. Here are some nationwide hotlines in the United States that can connect you to safety. Please reach out for assistance—you are worth it and you deserve the magickal life you were meant to live.

Gay, Lesbian, Bisexual and Transgender National Hotline: 1 (888) 843-4564

Department of Defense (DOD) Safe Helpline for Sexual Assault: 1 (877) 995-5247

National Runaway Safeline: 1 (800) 786-2929

ChildHelp National Child Abuse Hotline: 1 (800) 422-4453

National Alliance on Mental Illness (NAMI) Helpline: 1 (800) 950-6264

Foreword

In 2019 I heard from a Witch seeking to write for Patheos Pagan's *The Agora*. He wrote, "I'm interested in telling people how I fail, where I learned something, and my personal take on the witching world in general. I feel like there isn't really a voice out there saying, 'Hey I'm human and I mess up too. But check it out; I kept trying and these are the results I got.'"

Vincent Higginbotham's voice is unique among Pagan writers. His is a story of personal and magickal perseverance in the face of setback upon setback. With unflinching candor, Vincent shares his journey as a Witch in search of and finding his power, from his time as a child raised in an abusive home to his adolescence spent in foster care to his experiences of homelessness as a young gay man.

Vincent's essential message is not so much one of transcendence as it is a story of deep knowledge of who he is as a Witch, of understanding and working with the materials of his experiences to conjure the life he knew he wanted to have. In this book he lays everything on the table—the good, the bad, and the sometimes very ugly—and shares with his readers the magicks he employed to harness the energies around him so that they worked to his ultimate benefit.

Throughout these pages you will find tips and teachings to help you deal with many of the stumbling blocks life can throw your way, and the magickal workings you can manifest to address them. Each spell is explained in easy to understand steps and utilizes elements that are very affordable and easily accessible. Above all, these spells make magickal sense—you'll not only learn *how* they work; you'll be able to understand *why* they work.

If you're looking for pretty potion bottles and a high-gloss Hollywood Witch vibe, this is not the book for you. This book is gritty. It's practical. It's transformative. It's about a Witch who failed—failed so many more times than once—and yet never gave up on himself or his Craft. He persisted, and he achieved the results he wanted.

This is an extraordinary book about how witchcraft changed one man's life, and in its pages you will discover how magick can change your life as well.

Martha Kirby Capo, Editor of
Patheos Pagan's *The Agora*

Introduction

Magick in real life isn't all circles and rituals. It is often acts of desperation, performed out of need rather than want. Magick is used to protect ourselves, to heal, and to understand the world around us. It is a tool to improve our lives. In this book you will be provided with the information I wish I'd had when I was going through my trouble. This is practical knowledge that, had I known it then, could have improved my outcomes and averted the issues that followed.

What you're about to read is a piece of my life. I have learned that stories which contain the harsh realities of life don't always sit well with everyone. If you're one of those people, this is not the book for you. I have had some hard times, which are shared in every chapter. There are two reasons for this: I believe in the power of a Witch's pain because we can draw from it in order to learn lessons and empower our magick, and secondly, I am not alone in these experiences. Real trauma happens all the time, and those who write about magick too often gloss over it.

My Story: Before I Knew It Existed

I was five. The movie *Dr. Jekyll and Mr. Hyde* was playing on the television. It was an old version of the same story we've all come to know. All the other kids were outside playing. It was sunny and I wanted to be out there with them. Instead, I was inside, punished for not knowing how to tie my shoes. The curtains were pulled tight, blocking the sun, and the only light in the room was from the black and white movie I had no interest in watching.

Our babysitter had a son. He was probably eighteen, although I was too young to be able to guess his age at the time. To me he was an adult. He lay on the couch with his hand down his pants, watching the man on the screen live two lives. I remember an innate sense of discomfort. I did my best to find the monochromatic screenplay enthralling. I did anything I could in order to keep my eyes off of him.

He whispered my name, told me to come over. With his hand he shook his exposed flesh at me. He told me to taste him. He told me this was our game, that I shouldn't tell anyone. He showed me how to use my mouth in ways I didn't know I could. He taught me something I shouldn't have learned for at least another decade. That day, my babysitter's son stole something from me long before I knew it existed. But he gave me something in its place, something that would set the pace for the rest of my life.

This wasn't the last time I was the victim of a sexual predator. My life has been littered with the pain of sexual abuse. It was a pain I learned to harness, command, and claim as mine. Even before I knew how to tie my shoes, the first thing I learned in life was that I could live through horrible moments. I learned that even though a moment would stick with me forever, I could find a way to grow from it; I could grow strong from my tragedies and create magick out of my pain.

If I Had Known

In truth, it would be difficult to find anyone who hasn't experienced a tragedy of some kind. We would struggle to find a person who was free of disease, depression, addiction, poverty, abuse, or any other hardship. Unfortunately, those things are part of the human condition. Luckily, they are also fuel for self-improvement, inspiration for the wherewithal to withstand hardship, and a source of true power.

If I had known that the trauma and hardships you're about to read would inform the lessons that I deliver with them, I would never have been the tortured writer who developed the skills to produce this book. My journey had meaning because it started from a place where I was utterly lost. I needed to fear my situation. Knowing the good my trials would one day deliver to the world would have made them slightly more bearable, which would have robbed them of the experience they provided me.

There was a time when I didn't know how to protect myself. I wasn't aware of how to work with a deity. I was born into a fire, burnt at my very first breath. I continued to travel through that fire for decades. If I had known just half of what I know now, I may have exited that fire sooner. But that's not the point of the journey, is it? We exit our trials once we learn our lessons. This book is about those lessons. It's about the pain and the suffering I've known. It's about how what I know now about magick would have been a game-changer for me back then.

I made it through hell to come out stronger on the other side. If I had known then how to use the principles of magick that continued to present themselves to me all through my life, I would have had a much easier time on this path. I'm hopeful that through experiencing my journey and acquiring the knowledge I fought hard to learn, you won't suffer the way I had to.

Magick Is Our Birthright

When you're a practicing Witch, you are highly likely to meet Witches who will go on and on about how their mom is a Witch, and her mom was a Witch, and *her* mom's mom was as well. Often these hereditary Witches won't shy away from expressing their heritage—and they shouldn't. You may be one of these Witches yourself. I'm not, and that's okay too. The truth is, hereditary Witches aren't any more special than those of us who are not one. Their magick is just as hard won as ours. Witches know tragedy; they know hardship and struggle. There are Witches in the world who would have you believe otherwise. If they aren't lying about their lives or downplaying their real world experiences, then they're not as full of magick as they present themselves to be.

What makes all of us magickal, is our ability to bend the world to our will. What makes all of us special is the ingenuity of our human race. We evolve, we adapt, we manipulate the elements around us in order to get what we want. And that is the basics of Witchcraft. That is why magick is our birthright.

Witches combat their pain. They conquer their fear in order to manifest their desires. We know how energy works. And then we use our knowledge, our fear, and our pain to become stronger in a world that would see us defeated.

Pain Is Power

We all have pain. It is a normal and unremarkable thing for all humans everywhere. We have setbacks, let-downs, and betrayals. We have experienced abuse, marginalization, and bullies. The truth is that normally these behaviors are perpetrated by people who have experienced these actions themselves. A more simple truth is that hurt people hurt people. It's an endless cycle, like the ouroboros, a snake eating its own tail.

You're about to get to know me really well. I am choosing to allow you to see the vulnerable parts of me. I'm letting you in to see the things I don't really want to share with everyone. What I'm doing is something I've done my whole life, though. While I don't want to share this stuff, I do it because I know others need to know that they are not alone in this fight.

I can't hold on to the pain or suffering that I've known in my life, but I also can't pretend that it never happened or that it hasn't shaped everything about who I am today. Because if I did, I wouldn't be the powerful Witch who set out to write this book. Pain is power.

You may already be a Witch. We are all Witches if we choose to be; every one of us is magick. Every human possesses the power to manipulate the world around them in order to manifest both their desires, and their fears. It typically takes pain, trauma, hard knocks, and difficulties to really ignite that fire, though.

Some people come to Witchcraft out of desperation, at least initially. They need this or want that. Their religion or atheism weren't working for them so they took matters into their own hands. They turned to magick with the hope that maybe this would work. Maybe they were looking for acceptance, release, freedom, safety, prosperity, love, or who knows what else. Magick offers those things; it offers a way to work with the energies of a world that sometimes feels out of our control. Normally once we find our way to this path and choose to really travel it, we find so much more than just magick—we find our truth and our strength.

What You Can Expect

This book is about magick in real life. It's about looking at everyday things like the bills you have to pay, the job you hate, the sacrifices you make, and the trials you endure. It's about all that we humans have to put up with like abuse, neglect, poverty, loneliness, prejudice, and addiction. This book is about finding the magickal things that make life easier to deal with. It's about using that magick to alleviate our suffering.

You are going to get glimpses of my pain. Some of these snapshots might be hard to digest; others you will probably relate to. This is purposeful in each chapter. By sharing moments of my greatest pain I am able to then explain what I now understand about magick. I use my story as a springboard to dive into lessons on practical magick that can be used to empower and help pull any Witch up out of despair or hardship.

Throughout the book, you will find requests to *Try This*, *Suggested Reading*, and *Journal Prompts*. These are the points that notate where we are in a lesson.

The *Try This* sections offer a practice for you, the reader, to participate in. Magick is a practice after all so, dive in; give these things a shot.

Journal Prompts are just that—prompts for you to dig deeper into your own mind. Here I ask you to consider some aspect of a particular lesson and how it is present in your life. This is an excellent opportunity to develop your understanding of your own practice while solidifying your system of beliefs.

Finally, *Suggested Reading* will always list literature you can seek out to improve your understanding and development of the specific lesson taught in a chapter.

You might want to get yourself a notebook as a companion to reading this book. I share spells and practices that you are more than welcome to add to your own book of shadows. In fact, my book of shadows doesn't just contain spells and information on magickal things—it has a lot of personal journaling and lists of books that I have yet to read.

Whether you use a companion journal, compile a book of shadows as you read, or participate in any of the practice prompts is completely up to you. I believe there is no wrong way to Witch, and the same holds true with reading a book on Witchcraft.

Part One
LAYING THE FOUNDATION

In order to build anything a strong foundation is required, otherwise a structure will fail. Magick is no different in this regard. In this section I discuss the foundations of my magickal practice. There are nuances to anyone's practice and not all Witches build upon the same foundation. That is normal.

In part one I identify the things that have allowed me to become the Witch I am today. My practice is built upon an understanding of spiritual awareness—the magickal senses Witches are often gifted with—as well as the right to practice as I see fit, the ability to protect myself, the tarot, and the creation of strong spell work through the act of persistence in mundane ways. None of these lessons are meant to be rules but they got me to where I am today, so I know they can help any practitioner build their own practice into a formidable one.

1
The Spirits around Us

As big and dynamic as our physical world is, the spirit realm is infinitely larger. We all have guides, guardians, and ancestors, none of whom are malicious. On the other side of that spectrum there are lower, lesser beings which seem to be more nefarious than anything else.

Spirits, entities, ghosts, demons, shadow people, and any other supernatural thing that goes bump in the night have always left me feeling unsettled. The Witching world is full of mediums and ghost hunters. Finding comfort in interacting with the ethereal world isn't unusual for many Witches. The facts are that there are more Witches who welcome phantasmal communications than those who do not.

Boundaries are a vital aspect of Witchcraft. Knowing where your line is drawn is important. If you're like me, then the idea of ghosts doesn't sit well with you either. However, it's important not to close yourself off from all aspects of the spirit realm. Some entities are incredibly helpful on a Witch's journey. Identifying the beneficial from the hindering will greatly increase any Witch's practice.

My Story: Real World, Otherworldly Things

I met a devil in New Orleans. Daily at nap time he'd show up to walk back and forth on my windowsill. As a five year old it was terrifying. He had the body of a cherub, except instead of wings he had a tail and where there should have been a cute face, there was no face at all. He was a silhouette pacing between the window and the blinds.

As I played quietly with my stuffed animals, I refused to participate in the afternoon ritual of sleep. A little, blond boy with blue eyes imagining myself as a hero, saving the universe. I'd look up at the window, the afternoon sun shining through despite our roller blinds, and there he'd be, strolling to and fro. In those moments I'd transform from a champion into a coward, jumping in my bed and hiding under the covers until nap time was over.

It was a daily occurrence to avoid my room in the afternoon. I would pretend to fall asleep just before being sent off to rest. I would argue against being tired, and swear to behave, "Please let me stay downstairs," I'd beg. This always failed, followed by a slow ascent up the steps to my bedroom knowing what was coming next.

In exile (so my babysitter could have a break), I would play, avoiding glancing at my window; full of hope that each day would be different. Eventually one was. I was sitting on my bed; there was movement in my window as the silhouette of the little demon began his daily journey inside the frame.

I was finished with the idea of living in fear at nap time. Anger permeated my actions. Standing up on my bed, fueled by rage, I mustered up all my emotion and told him, "You can't be here! I don't want you!" Then I added, "GO AWAY!"

With that, the small shadow being stopped pacing my windowsill. He turned his tiny body to face me, then reached his baby arm up. He grabbed a handful of the roller blinds, the only thing that stood between me and him. And then he yanked the shade out of the window.

The blinds lay on the floor and the devil stood there exposed. My tormentor, still only a silhouette. A shadow form, so dense I could not see through it.

I heard, "What was that?" called up from downstairs. I knew I was moments from safety. This thing, blacker than any darkness I'd ever seen, just stood there. He didn't have eyes but I felt him stare at me. The babysitter came running up the stairs, "What's going on up here?" She yelled on her way. As she burst through the door she said, "What did you do?"

Crying like only a five year old full of adrenaline can, I pointed to the window and said, "The devil did it." I was so relieved that someone else would finally see him. Turning back to the window expecting to confirm what I was saying, the devil was gone.

The whole scenario looked suspicious to the babysitter. Vinyl blinds were on the floor, there were holes in the wall where the shade was once anchored. The only visible culprit as far as she could tell, was me. I was still crying, still insisting that the devil did it. She grabbed me by the arm and pulled me to the hallway.

As punishment, the babysitter did what she usually did if she thought I was lying: she put toothpaste on my tongue until I told the truth. This time I would not break. I knew what I experienced. I knew that the devil was in my room. But I also knew she wouldn't believe me. Eventually, she let me rinse my mouth and go to bed. The devil never showed up again.

I don't know exactly what that devil was. As far as I can tell, this was a real experience. There is no amount of logic that can explain it, and what followed next would only confirm the reality of my shadow devil's existence.

After the liberation from baby Satan, I started seeing another type of shadowy figure. I'd be going about my day like any normal kid playing or reading, and then out of the corner of my eye, I would see movement. I'd turn to look only to catch what seemed like a shadow scurrying away.

I could be anywhere and catch one of these shadow things stalking me. Through intuition, I felt their presence long before seeing them. I'd always fight the urge to turn and look. Then I'd try my hardest to get a good glimpse without them knowing. This never worked. They would flutter off the moment I noticed them, even when I wasn't obvious about it. For years this was my secret.

Ten-year-olds don't normally attempt suicide, but I've never considered myself normal. The short story is, my big sister caught me. She saved my life and I ended up in a hospital for a while. There were so many doctors asking questions like, "Why do you want to die?" They'd ask, "What's going on in your life?" I explained that I didn't know, I just wasn't like everyone else.

Eventually a doctor came in and asked if I ever saw things that others couldn't. I opened up about the devil of New Orleans and then about the shadow things that ran from me. This created a whole new situation. These doctors thought I was hallucinating, but I knew better. Even then, I knew that what I was experiencing was real, that I was under some sort of spiritual attack. After a series of tests, it was decided that therapy was in order. This would be the beginning of a mental health journey that continues to this day.

My first therapist suggested that I start telling the shadow people to go away. As it turns out, this worked. Similar to telling the baby devil to leave me alone, I took authority and the shadows left. Thankfully they didn't ruin any blinds on their way out of my life.

If I Had Known

If I had known as a child that other people were having experiences like this, I might not have felt so alone. I might not have felt crazy. What I know now is that the baby devil and the shadowy blurs I saw are a real phenomenon. Seeing shadow people is something that has since been studied and discussed publicly for a while. It has been linked to both sleep paralysis and sleep deprivation. There have been books written on the matter that suggest the experience could be anything from demonic attacks to extra-dimensional interactions. The media has even included these entities in television and film.

But in the eighties, when I was growing up, none of this was mainstream knowledge. Had it been, I would have been able to learn better how to deal with the situation. But the advice I received was "just ignore it," and "tell them to go away." There was no standard practice on dealing with something others couldn't see. There wasn't a prescribed way of protecting myself. To the professionals, I was just some kid with mental issues. And yeah, sure, I was, but this wasn't that. This was the spirit realm attempting to communicate with me in ways I was neither ready for nor want to participate in.

Had I known then that what I was having were spiritual experiences and that I had a say in the role I played in these interactions, I could have put a stop to things sooner. I would have created boundaries or raised my vibration.

Magick was very much not a part of my life yet, so instead I prayed to Jesus. I understood my experience as a demonic attack, while others viewed it as attention seeking or mental instability. There wasn't an internet for me to search and learn, though I was too young to do so even if it did exist. I couldn't learn that other people were having the same encounters as me. I was alone, left to believe that what was happening to me was anything but legitimate. If I had known that I could one day have the power to handle this sort of thing, I would have tried to learn, even if I was too young to understand.

The facts are that regardless of what these things I saw were, I was able to send them away. I don't believe that they were symptoms of sleep issues but rather spiritual encounters meant to shake me to my core. If I had an understanding of the Source I might have tapped into it in those moments. We all vibrate at different energetic levels and, what I know now is that beings like the ones I experienced attack those who are vibrating at lower levels.

Creating Boundaries

When we are young, it is easier to be open to energies and ideas. For this reason, many children become beacons to the unseen world. When left unguarded, anything could find its way to them. Children tend to be more accepting of what adults often find hard to believe; they can become open doors that many entities find inviting. And because it is rare for a child to know how to protect themselves from unwanted spirit contact, entities seek them out more often.

People need boundaries. As a Witch, I choose how to interact with the spirit realm. It is necessary for us to close our metaphoric door and only allow access to those beings we want to interact with. Though it takes work to set those boundaries firmly, it is important that we are the ones who make the call on whatever we experience. Creating boundaries is how we do that.

Before setting boundaries, it is important to see the big picture. The spirit realm exists whether we can see it or not, and most people aren't even aware of it. This is why when a spirit realizes it can connect with us, it latches on. Suddenly a neglected, unseen entity receives the attention it had been starved for. Recognizing the power we give them with our attention is the first step to developing ramparts they cannot break through. In other words, you are in control because it is your attention they are seeking. When you make a firm decision on how you will accept their contact, you are making the rules.

JOURNAL PROMPT
Deciding Your Boundaries

In your journal, make a list of what is and is not okay for you in terms of spirit contact. When is it okay for a spirit or entity to interact with you? Do you want to see them, hear them, or feel their presence? Write out all your limits on one side of the page and then list all acceptable forms of interaction on the other side.

You can go so far as to list times when you will and will not accept contact. Maybe the shower is off limits for you but your drive to work is acceptable. Be as thorough as possible so it will help you maintain healthy boundaries with the spirit world. After you have created your lists, write out your specific intentions and then move on to the exercise that follows.

TRY THIS
Setting Your Boundaries

Make a firm decision on what is and is not okay with you in terms of spirit contact. You can do this verbally or in your mind. If you want to see spirits, make a statement that it is okay that they present themselves visually. If seeing the spirit realm is unsettling to you but hearing them is fine, say that. Some people don't mind seeing or hearing things that others cannot. If neither of these forms of interaction are of interest to you, make a clear statement that this is the case.

You can set the intention that your only acceptable form of spirit interaction is through signs or symbols. If this is the case, decide what signs are allowed. You can make any boundary you like. For example, if you only wish to receive contact through media like songs or statements on the radio and television, let that be known. A statement such as, "It is okay if the hair on the back of my neck stands up when I am receiving a message through a line in a song," tells the spirit world where your definitive line of acceptance is.

Enforce your boundaries. You will be tested. When an entity shows up outside of your boundaries, it is up to you to reaffirm your rules. For example, if you have told them you don't want to see them and they appear visually, you have to tell them no. Don't give them attention outside of saying, "No, this is breaking my rules. I will not accept it." Make it clear that you don't want the contact when you receive it. Likewise, if an entity tests your boundaries, be firm. Say out loud, "I will not allow contact like this. If you want to interact, you can present yourself as a cold chill when someone I am speaking to makes a statement you want me to know." After giving clear instructions, stop. Do not give the entity any more energy after that.

The Source

All of creation is held together by energy. This energy is literally the force keeping your atoms and subatomic particles together, like a vibration that attracts all the pieces to each other. The book or device you're holding, the chair you're sitting in, the earth, and our entire universe; there is a pulse, much like our heartbeats, that keeps all those things tangible on this physical plane. That is what is binding everything together and it is the Source.

Inside everything: my dog, the wheels on my truck, the sun, paper, trees, and everything physical is the Source. Jesus, Hekate, Odin, the Universe, Hermes, Pele, Ganesha, and literally any other deity I could list—all are the same thing, the Source. Or rather, they are a part of it, fragmented into egregores and ultimately powered by the beliefs of the humans who conceived them and continue to honor their existence.

The Source is the beginning of everything. It is where our consciousness exists before we are born. It is where our minds return when we die. It is the dynamic frequency that all vibrations fall into. The Source is neither light nor dark, it isn't good or bad; it doesn't fall somewhere on a scale, because it *is* the scale, and it contains every energetic and physical entity in existence. This one thing is fragmented and multiplied an infinite number of times. Angels and demons, deities, guides, guardians, sound, dark matter and stars, atoms, molecules, and diseases are all the Source. And we humans are part of the Source, too.

As members of this divine, singular thing, we have a say. We have the ability to choose our interaction with everyone else. In other words, a ghost or a guide is just a part of us—even though it is separated and experiencing the world from its own subjective view, it shares universal consciousness nonetheless. All the pieces that make up the Source have a vibration. Understanding this is the key to setting boundaries as well as accessing magick in general.

Understand Your Vibration

Your vibration is an indicator of where you fall in the spectrum that makes up the Source. It does not dictate the level of your connection but rather the frequency of communication you are open to. In other words, the vibration of the entities we interact with are going to closely resemble our own. If you have experienced a lot of trauma and are stuck in a victim mentality, you are more likely to have low vibrational beings attaching themselves to you and leading you into situations that feed your belief that you are a victim.

Humans are dynamic in our emotions. Our highs can soar beyond imagination and our lows run deep. In between those extremes is a large gray area. It is there that we spend the most time. No one is always happy any more than anyone is always angry; there are fluctuations in our moods, and the same holds true for our vibration.

Likewise, people don't all fall into one frequency; rather, there is a spectrum for each individual. We are all unique and each of us will find ourselves at a different location on the scale of vibration. That said, there is a baseline or starting point—an average range that we tend to hover around with fluctuations that depend on our current situation.

A child born into the quintessentially stable family might have a much different starting point from one born into a less-than-ideal family. This doesn't mean that either child will remain in those vibrational ranges, however. As the journey down the path continues, similar circumstances will affect everyone differently. Where one person could have an alcoholic parent and choose to never touch substances of any sort, another could make the opposite choice and fall into addiction themselves.

It bears repeating that none of us will remain at the same vibrational point as the one at which we start. How could we? As we grow, we go through so many things that develop us into the adults we become. This is why something that affects us as children seems to affect us less when it happens to us as adults. We might not deal with things in the healthiest of ways but we learn to cope as we grow, thus setting our personal spectrum of vibrations.

When you understand your vibration, you are able to effectively identify how you're connected to the Source and all its varied entities. This understanding is essential in taking the first step to setting your boundaries. If you know you're vibrating at a lower frequency, that awareness alone is the first step to helping you begin to level up.

One of the best ways to become aware of your vibration is by being aware of your thoughts. What we think sets our vibration whether we intend for it to or not. In order to change our vibrations, we must first be aware of them. This takes daily practice but eventually you'll find that changing the way you think will change your interactions with the world around you.

JOURNAL PROMPT
What Thoughts Lower Your Vibration?

In your journal, write about the pain you are holding onto, whether it is abuse or heartbreak. Dive deep into the things that have hurt you in the past. Try to connect to the instances from your past that have led to, for example, your need to always be right, or to feel as though you are on the defensive all the time. You can write about your pain as a story of what happened, or a poem. You could also write free associations about feelings of neglect or shame, or you could write a song about feeling isolated or lonely as a child.

Writing these things out is a great first step to ridding your life of the feelings they cause. Once you can see them on paper, you are likely to be able to identify them better when they are causing your vibration to be lowered.

Vibrational Beings

While my initial interactions with the spirit realm were with low vibration entities, it is important to note that much higher vibrational beings exist as well. On the low end of the spectrum, beings feed off of pain and negative emotions. Entities on the higher side are empowered by positive and uplifting energies. Learning the difference between the two will help to limit our interactions with entities we would rather not engage.

My childhood was full of trauma from sexual abuse. This abuse caused my energies to vibrate at a lower frequency, which opened the door for low-level entities to begin tormenting me. The shadow figures induced fear and shame, the same feeling that being molested caused in me; the two experiences go hand in hand. However, this doesn't mean that everyone who has seen a shadow person was sexually abused. It is more likely that the feelings a shadow being elicit in the viewer mirrors some other feeling they are experiencing.

Because I was young and unarmed with the skills to fight off these beings, they attached themselves to me and thereby created a cycle in which the same form of abuse continued to happen. It wasn't until I was ten and instructed to send the shadows away that sexual abuse ended in my life. The beings were basically fed by my emotions in two ways: they were able to feed off of the feelings the abuse created in me, and they then created similar feelings in me they were able to feed off of as well. They gained power and more control by engaging with me in the cat-and-mouse game we played, which was their way of ensuring that I stayed at a low vibration. Keeping me in the mindset of shame and isolation allowed them to interact with me. They gained my attention and it made them stronger, thus enabling them to continue their attacks.

On the other side of the spectrum are high vibrational beings. These entities want good things for us and often guide us toward our true purpose. They interact with us in the same way as the lower beings do, gently guiding us along our path. When we are more in tune with ourselves, it is easier to follow their lead. As always, awareness is the key to following these higher beings. Being aware lets us hear or feel these beings' counsel. And when we follow their direction, we create a stronger connection to them, thus allowing clearer information to come through. We empower these entities with our higher-level emotions like trust and gratitude.

While high and low vibration entities both feed off of our interactions with them, the differences between the two are significant. Lower beings find comfort in negative emotions and interaction. The opposite is true for the higher beings: even though we fluctuate within the large spectrum of human emotion, we make a choice (albeit often subconsciously) as to where our baseline vibration rests. Therefore in order to lessen or enhance our connections with either end of this dichotomy, we must remain conscious and strive to make the decisions that align with the boundaries we set.

Our vibrations and the entities we are prone to interact with are in an ever changing state. Where you are today is not likely the same place you will find yourself a few years from now. When we find ourselves vibrating in the lower range, we are faced with the option to make a change, whether it is to become more optimistic, speak up for ourselves, or anything else that could help us to raise our vibration.

TRY THIS
Raising Your Vibration

Are you constantly degrading yourself? In any potential situation, do you focus on the possible negative outcomes?

When you catch yourself thinking in more negative ways, stop yourself. Take a moment to acknowledge the thought you've had, and then push it out of your mind by replacing it with a more positive idea. For instance, you might think that while it is *possible* that the whole world will burn, it is unlikely that will happen. Remind yourself when you have a negative thought that there is a positive, opposite one to be had as well.

Next time you are worried about your bills, health, or whatever it is that occupies your mind, allow the thought. Afterward, take the time to think of five things that are not negative in regard to what it is that worries you. You could say, "I don't know how I will make my car payment this month," but follow it up with, "I've been making my car payment so far, it will work itself out."

As you move forward from those negative thoughts, begin to stop allowing them. At this point you have already started to train yourself to think of the positive ideas also. Instead of saying, "I'm sick and probably dying," say things like, "I'm not feeling great, but I'll feel better soon."

Rephrase whatever it is that you are thinking of negatively into a new positive idea. Acknowledge the truth of the situation and then expect the most positive of outcomes. This is one way to actively work on raising your vibration every day.

Suggested Reading

Mediumship: An Introductory Guide to Developing Spiritual Awareness and Intuition by Gordon Smith. Hay House, 2017.

Egregores: The Occult Entities That Watch Over Human Destiny by Mark Stavish. Inner Traditions, 2018.

2
Magickal Senses

The majority of us possess five senses: tasting, feeling, smelling, seeing, and hearing. Some people see better than they hear, and others lack one of these senses altogether. It is commonly known that when we are blocked off from one sense, the others tend to pick up the slack. The fact alone that we can experience the world with these five abilities is amazing, although they are often taken for granted. In the Witching world, we are aware of a special sixth sense that the mundane tends to overlook.

This sixth sense is like a special power. It tends to be as unique as each of us are, and it isn't actually something only Witches possess. I call this our magickal sense. More commonly known as clairsense, this is an extra sensory ability that most everyone is born with. While these senses present themselves in different ways the origin of these gifts all come from the same place, our connection to the Source.

Have you ever known the phone was about to ring before it did? Or have you had a feeling something was wrong even though you had no reason to feel that way? These are examples of clair-sense. It is like the Source's way of communicating to us what is or is about to happen.

Just like we learn to use our basic five senses we must develop an understanding for our clairsense as well. None of us were born knowing what a bell sounds like or that the color we are seeing is called blue—we learn to identify those things as we grow. In this same way, our magickal senses must be learned and identified in order to gain the benefits they provide.

My Story: I Want to Be Super

I remember watching a movie in which a woman gets married to a butcher. When she moves home with him, she meets the town-ies and their local therapist. The woman is also a psychic, so the therapist tries to shrink her head because he is a rational skeptic. Hilarity ensues as a little romance and drama develop. Eventu-ally, the main character leaves the butcher for the therapist after she proves herself as a psychic and the two fall in love.

Sorry if I spoiled that for you.

Throughout the movie, various characters call the main char-acter "clairvoyant." As a ten-year-old viewing this movie for the first time, I was confused. The character's name was Maria or something like that, and I remember thinking, "Who is this 'Clair Voyant' everyone keeps talking about, and why do these people think Maria is her?" I sat through the whole movie wait-ing to find out who this Clair lady was! I didn't understand why the main character didn't know her real name was Clair.

After the movie ended, my sister and I walked out of the movie theater. But to me, the mystery of Clair's identity was still completely unsolved. I asked my sister, "Who's Clair Voyant?"

"What?" she replied.

I asked again, "Who is Clair Voyant?"

"What are you talking about?"

"In the movie," I said. "They kept calling her Clair Voyant. Who is that?"

I was so confused by the whole thing, but my sister laughed at me and rolled her eyes. "It means she was psychic," she explained.

I thought to myself, "Why didn't they just say that?"

Afterward, I wanted to learn more. Honestly, I wanted to *be* more; for as long as I can remember, I've been fascinated by supernatural gifts. The idea of having power really amazed me, and I'm willing to bet it's what amazes all of us. Being more special than our next-door neighbor is definitely a drawing point. Everybody wants to feel special, and especially as children, it's common for us to search for our own specialness. For many Witches, it is likely this very search that led us to our path.

The idea that clairvoyance was potentially attainable amazed my young mind. I wanted something bigger and was determined to figure out how to get it. I sought out knowledge. Unfortunately, the elementary school library held very little resources for such an endeavor. There was some information to be found, but none of it was the answer I was really searching for.

I learned about ESP and remote viewing from what I could find in the library at school. I pored over books that were barely understandable. With the hopes of unlocking some innate talent for hearing a person's innermost thoughts, my consumption of information became an obsession. There were yes or no tests to identify how psychic the reader was. I lied my way through them in order to convince myself that I too could see the future.

If I Had Known

The dream of developing a gift, even just a mild sense of clairvoyance, was real to me. Eventually, though, hope was lost—the real world bled into my youthful worldview and in its place grew false understanding. I began to believe that I would never have these types of gifts because they were just fiction. If I had known that abilities present themselves much differently in the real world than they do in the movies, I would have held onto that hope and begun developing my clairsenses much sooner.

It's not unusual to experience these clairsenses because, in truth, we all possess one or more of them. What I didn't know is that fiction exaggerates the truth. It makes our natural psychic gifts appear fantastic. We are led to believe that these abilities are considered supernatural, but they are not. In fact, they are so natural that we often fail to recognize these gifts in our lives. Clairsenses are our intuition. While they may not play out the way the media tends to exaggerate them, they are definitely a superpower worth developing.

Clairsenses

The word *clair* means clear. It's the French masculine form of the word. When used in regard to the clairsenses, we are basically saying *clear senses*. And though they are called clear, that is not always the case. It often takes a lot of effort to learn to discern between a true clairsense moment and a random thought, scent, feeling, sound, or taste. Defining these senses as clear has more to do with how we experience the sense once we have learned to truly identify them.

Clairsenses are intuitive senses. They can manifest in connection to one or more of our five basic senses. Some people experience this phenomenon in multiple ways, while others specifically use only one. The information and number of clairsenses varies widely. There are some who identify only four of these gifts while others can enumerate at least eight extra sensory abilities. I find that there are six solid clairsenses that cover the full expanse of our intuitive sense spectrum.

Clairvoyance is connected to our ability to see. Clairaudience works in conjunction with our sense of hearing. Claircognizance, which has to do with knowing, doesn't so much coincide with one of our five senses but it is a highly intuitive aspect of these magickal senses nonetheless. Clairsentience comes through our sense of feeling. Clairgustance works with our ability to taste, and clairalience is connected to our sense of smell.

Clairvoyance

Clairvoyant is not a lady's name but rather an interesting gift to have. It is the ability to use intuition to see with the mind events that are taking place in the present, took place in the past, or will take place in the future.

This is the most widely known of the clairsenses. This specific gift is often depicted in television and film. In the popular American television show *Charmed*, Phoebe Halliwell is gifted with this ability. Albeit exaggerated for dramatic purposes, it is a strong depiction of one of the clairsenses, though clairvoyance is much more subtle than seen on film.

Think about picturing your dream house: envision the green shutters against the rough-sawn cedar siding. Clairvoyance is like this—clearly seeing in the mind. Maybe what comes through is a color; you see it as vividly as your own hand. It is like a sudden flash in your vision, then the phone rings. Your mom is on the line telling you about her new Toyota Camry, and you already know the car is champagne colored.

Imagination is a key indicator of this talent. Not everyone is able to see a clear picture of what is in their head; visualization is difficult for many. That doesn't mean it's impossible though.

TRY THIS
See the Object

Practice with your imagination. Take some time each day and sit alone. Remove distractions from your environment. To develop visualization, it helps to pick one thing to see in your mind. Grab something you are familiar with: your favorite pen, a cup, or anything close by. It helps if the item you choose to practice with is something you use on a daily basis and are already accustomed to what it looks like.

First, study the object. Take time to memorize the details of whatever it is you have chosen to focus on. Now close your eyes. Make the effort to see the object in your mind. Envision the curves and angles that create its shape. Open your eyes and study the object again. Take notice of just a small part of it. When you close your eyes again, try to see just one detail you were memorizing. Throughout your day, see if you can recall the object.

Over time and with a great deal of practice, you will likely reach a point where seeing the item in your mind's eye comes easy for you. Doing this will help you exercise your visualization muscles, and eventually you will find that visualization can also help with a lot of other magickal practices beyond clairvoyance.

Note: There are people in the world who cannot visualize things. Do not become discouraged if this practice isn't easy for you. If you struggle with visualizing things, that's okay. You probably have a much stronger, different clairsense ability readily available to tap into.

Clairaudience

Not everyone experiences clairvoyance. Sometimes a person hears precognitive messages instead of seeing them. When we hear things in our head, like our thoughts, we are hearing through what is typically called the mind's ear. The ability to receive messages in this way is called clairaudience.

When you're sorting out a problem in your mind and then out of nowhere you hear the solution, this is clairaudience. Maybe the voice you heard was not the same one you think with. What's happening is that your internal dialogue is being accessed by your intuition, almost as if someone else snuck into your head and spoke up.

Imagine you are having money problems. You start trying to figure out how to make ends meet. As you are mulling the situation over, you hear, "Let's check the job listings for a gig." After following the advice from inside your mind, you find the perfect part-time opportunity. It makes exactly the amount you need and it's definitely a job you can do while maintaining your day job. Was that your idea? Did you say that to yourself? Or were you led to the idea by your own clairaudience?

Intuition is in fact a tricky thing to learn to pay attention to. People spend lifetimes attempting to hone in on this sixth sense in all its forms. Clear hearing in particular can be difficult to discern. We think all day, and those of us who think with our internal dialogue hear ourselves while we think. Identifying the difference between our own thoughts and the ones we receive as a message takes some work. But when we pay close attention to our thoughts, we will find that the voice we hear when experiencing clairaudience is quite different from our own.

TRY THIS
Listen for the Source

Find a quiet place and set your intention to hear a message from the Source. Sit in silence and listen to all the sounds around you—the wind, birds, ocean, or even cars passing on the streets nearby. Begin to ignore all the outer noise you are hearing. Listen inwardly. What comes through in your mind's ear?

Hone in on what appears in your internal dialogue in this moment. Write down anything that comes through and then refer back to it later to see if it was an intuitive message from the Source.

TRY THIS
The Message in Music

Sometimes the messages we receive can be filtered through the sense our ability is connected to. If you listen to digital music, grab the device you use and set it to shuffle. Set the intention to receive a message through the first song that plays. Hit the next button as many times as you would like and press stop when you are ready. What song is playing? Does it relate to anything relative in your present situation?

JOURNAL PROMPT
The Things You Heard

Keep your journal with you as you go through your day. In it, make a list of the internal dialogue you hear in your head. Take notes on anything that sounds different from your own inner dialogue. If the thoughts do sound different, what do they say? Does anything sound like something you know or a message you need to hear?

When practicing either of the exercises above, mark your journal with the date and time. Record anything that comes through from them as well. As you write out the things you heard, see if anything else starts to come through. This is the time to let your internal dialogue speak, and it is often easier to hear your clairaudience while writing.

Practice this ability as often as you can. Eventually you will learn to recognize the difference between your own inner voice and that of messages received from the Source.

Claircognizance

The innate sense of knowing something intuitively without prior knowledge can be both amazing and frustrating. This gift will drive you crazy if you let it. Second-guessing your intuition because there is no clear indication aside from just *knowing* is a common occurrence with claircognizance.

Say you're in a conversation with your best friend, who is going on and on about being single. She tells you it's been months since she's been intimate with anyone. You look at her sympathetically, but in that moment you know she is pregnant. It isn't exactly a thought that runs through your head; it isn't a vision either. You just *know* but shrug it off because she just said that she hasn't had sex in ages. All the while, deep down you are sure something is up, because you can't let go of the idea that there is in fact a child growing inside her.

Three days later, your friend calls you in a panic. Her period is late and she took a test. It turns out she's pregnant. Obviously you ask her how that is possible. She explains that there was this one drunken night with a mutual friend. It was just a hookup, she tells you. She barely remembers it. Your friend admits she lied.

Claircognizance is a pretty awesome way to receive intuitive messages. The overwhelming clarity with which you know a message is true is part of the gift. Clear knowing leaves very little room for doubt.

You may find yourself having self-doubt as you come into your ability. One of the best ways to combat doubt when perfecting this clairsense is to keep notes.

JOURNAL PROMPT
Write What You Know

When you have a knowing of anything at all, stop and write it down in your journal. Doing this will give you something you can look back on when your claircognizance proves itself to be accurate. Over time, recording and reviewing will build your trust in your own clairsense; eventually, you won't feel the need to write down every claircognizant message.

Clairsentience

Picture yourself out walking your dog. You're going with the flow and have decided to let him lead you where he may. You realize you are in a part of the neighborhood that you don't normally go into. Walking down the street, you get a tight feeling in your gut. It feels like a warning but the neighborhood is pretty safe so you figure maybe it is something else. Continuing to walk, up ahead there are blue flashing lights. An ambulance is in the distance and getting closer. Some guy is running full force right at you, and behind him two cops are yelling at him to stop.

The street is big enough for two cars to pass each other. To the right there are bushes perfect for hiding. With the dog in tow, you duck into a cavity in the hedges, hidden from the pursuit unfolding down the road. One of the cops tackles the runner to the ground. The tightness in your gut is still there but as the officers handcuff the guy, it begins to subside.

Clairsentience is a psychic feeling of what is happening or what is about to happen. It's like walking into danger and feeling a visceral reaction. This sense can also inform us of what is happening for others as well. You might get light headed and dizzy at the same moment your father knocks himself out on the other side of town. Or your heart might begin to race as your sister starts to have an anxiety attack. Clairsentience can present several other ways as well, such as that chill you get up your spine on a hot summer day or the painful cramp you suddenly get for no reason. These can all be the manifestation of the gift to feel intuitively.

The great thing about clairsentience is that once you are aware of it, it's easy to discern when you're experiencing it. Because it is a feeling, there tends to be very little questioning involved. Most people already associate instinct with their gut feelings. For that reason alone, it is the easiest clairsense to hone in on.

TRY THIS
What Feelings Are Others Stirring in You?

Start by paying attention to your body. Does it react differently around different people? Do you feel anxious for no reason around your sister-in-law or excited when your niece is around? These feelings could be your physical reaction to other people's moods and emotions.

Pay attention to the feelings you get from the people around you. Simply put, trusting your feelings is the best way to practice and tap into the ability of clairsentience. As you develop trust in your feelings, you will find that they are feeding you information all the time. The more you pay attention to your feelings, the more you will be able to acknowledge what they are trying to help you understand.

JOURNAL PROMPT
What Does Your Gut Say?

When you have a gut reaction to anything, make a note in your journal about the feelings you are having. You don't need to be able to explain why you are having the reaction, just writing it down when you feel anxious for no reason will help you see later how you were receiving messages throughout your day. When you take the time to look back over your journal you are likely to find clarity on the feelings you had.

Clairgustance

You may have heard the saying "it puts a bad taste in my mouth." For people with the gift of clairgustance, that experience can often be literal. As odd as it may sound, the ability is real and many people experience it.

Clairgustance is the clairsense of taste. It allows a person to sense flavors that aren't present but are relevant to the intuitive message they are receiving. The clairsensitive person does not need to be eating or drinking anything in order to experience this. All they need is to be tuned into their intuition and paying attention to their taste buds.

Imagine you've spent the week craving french toast. Whenever you think about this particular breakfast food, your sister always comes to mind. The weekend comes around. You've wanted french toast so badly all week that your mouth waters with the thought of it. On Saturday morning while preparing to satisfy the craving, the phone rings. It's your sister.

The one person in the world who you associate french toast with calls at the exact moment the breakfast is ready to be cooked. As it turns out she is in town. She was only supposed to be there for a quick meeting yesterday but her flight was delayed until this afternoon. She has time now and wants to know if you'd like to get brunch near the airport with her.

In this example, clairgustance was telling you that you may interact with your sister. Now on Saturday morning, she is asking you to go to brunch. She will likely order the french toast. You're thinking you'd like eggs because the craving and taste for french toast has left your mouth.

TRY THIS
Taste More Things

Expanding the diversity of your palate will help to inform this gift. Experiment with different tastes, try new spices and textures to create an in-depth catalog of flavors. A better catalog of flavors will help you identify what you are tasting. And when you can identify what you taste, you can understand the messages you receive more clearly.

Clairalience

The gift of clairalience is the sense of clear smelling, or receiving intuitive messages through our sense of smell. Much like clairgustance with tastes, clairalience works through sensing scents and aromas that are not present. In this instance, a fragrance could remind us of something that is connected to an event in the past, present, or future.

Sometimes clairalience can be an early indicator of something. As with any clairsense, it can come in handy when loved ones are in trouble.

At home, hamburgers are cooking on the skillet. The fragrance of garlic, salt, pepper, and other spices used to make those delicious patties of meat fills the whole house. Suddenly, an intense scent begins assaulting your nostrils. Nothing you're cooking should smell this way. It brings to mind a chemical but it's sweet. You are reminded of a broken-down car on the side of the road. You feel alarmed and start frantically looking around for what you've set on fire, but nothing is burning.

Instead, maybe you feel a sudden flash of intuition. There is a sense that you should call your mom. When you do call her, she discloses that she had an issue with her engine today. Her power steering line had a pinhole in it and every time she turned her car it shot fluid all over her engine block. There was smoke and an odor. She's fine, the line is fixed, and she's glad you checked on her.

TRY THIS
What's That Smell?

Random scents flow into our nostrils all day. Take time to identify each one. Do you smell fast food when there isn't any in sight? This could be a message from the Source. It could also be the person next to you who has a bag of delicious food. Paying attention to our surroundings is imperative for identifying clairalience. The things we smell could often have a natural source, even if we can't identify a point of origin. Noticing the difference will soon expand your understanding of clairalience while helping you decipher the meaning of the messages you receive.

JOURNAL PROMPT
What Does It Bring to Mind?

When you smell something, let it trigger your memories. Pay close attention to what it might mean. The best way to keep track of these experiences is to write them all down in your journal. Describe the scents that come to you whether they seem mundane or not. List the feelings they bring up. If you are able to locate where they are coming from, mention that as well. When you can't find the source of a smell, focus on what the meaning could be and feel with your intuition to see if there is deeper meaning behind the scent. After a month has passed, read over what you have compiled. How often did a scent predict something that came up in your daily life?

Sometimes One Isn't Enough

Often the clairsenses will play off of each other. I may have a moment of knowing followed by a tingle at the base of my skull (claircognizance and clairsentience working in concert). You could be in a dangerous situation and get a visceral reaction while hearing a message that you should leave, which would be clairsentience teaming up with clairaudience.

Just the other day while driving to work, I had this "knowing" that my position needed to start a half hour earlier than everyone else. As the claircognizance occurred, I heard the voice of my boss in my head telling me this was the case. Then a tingle ran all over my head. When I got to work, the very first thing my boss said to me was "Vini, I think we're going to need you to start coming in at seven instead of seven thirty." This was claircognizance in combination with clairaudience as well as clairsentience—a moment of knowing followed by an internally audible message that was combined with a physical reaction to both. This is the most surefire way to identify a clairsense moment. I didn't have some random passing thought. The three senses informed me and then were immediately followed by confirmation that the experience was real. My intuition was preparing me for an important conversation. Because my clairsenses kicked in, I was able to consider my feelings on the matter before my boss brought it up.

Sometimes one sense isn't enough. When we pay close attention to our clairsenses we will find that they often interact with each other. This is an experience that confirms our psychic intuition is at work.

TRY THIS
Is There More Than One?

When you feel like you are having a clairsense moment, pay close attention to all your other senses. If you're smelling something, is there a feeling that comes with it? If you're feeling something, do you get a taste in your mouth as well? For a lot of Witches, this is often the case.

As we grow our gifts, it is likely we will find that they are working together. Being able to quickly identify when one sense is feeding another will help us to identify the message and quickly understand what is being presented to us.

Learning to Listen

If you've ever played a sport or an instrument, you know it takes practice to become great at it. No one wakes up one morning knowing how to play the piano. While there have been cases of people picking up the skill at ridiculous speeds, those are few and far between. The clairsenses are no different.

Learning to use your clairsense takes time and a lot of practice. Some of us have a natural affinity to using our senses. My son, for instance, showed a lot of skill in clairalience when he was a toddler. He would walk into people's houses and tell us he didn't like the smell. Meanwhile there was not a noticeable scent. He'd say things like "this place smells like death" often in places that my husband and I also didn't want to be.

The magick of this behavior is that my son didn't know what he was doing. He was simply reacting to a sense. It was natural and he perceived it as normal. He was a blank slate at the time, instinctively listening to his intuition. He hadn't yet learned self-doubt. It wasn't until he got older that we noticed he stopped walking into places and mentioning what he smelled. Somewhere along the way, his gift either stopped presenting itself or he stopped listening to it. One day when he is older, it is possible that he will rekindle this gift.

What's most important about developing your clairsenses is paying attention to your intuition. Even if it seems crazy; even if you feel as though what you think, feel, smell, taste, hear, or envision is way off, lean into it. Speak up if you want. Give your intuition a chance to be right every time you feel it. And when you're wrong, make a mental note about how that moment was different from when you were right. The more you do this, the more you will learn to decipher the difference between the two. Eventually you will have a clear understanding of your intuition and the ways in which the Source communicates with you.

There is a caveat to using our gifts as well. Ethically speaking, it is not always appropriate to tell others about the messages we receive in regard to them. As is the case with anything, just because we know something doesn't mean we should say something. It is possible to receive messages about people who are not looking for a psychic impression on the matter. If you have not been asked for your opinion, it is best to keep the information you glean to yourself.

JOURNAL PROMPT
What Clairsense Are You Experiencing?

Journaling can be an awesome tool in helping to connect to your intuition and clairsenses. By writing down different experiences we can begin to see a pattern. Start by taking some time and thinking about when your clairsenses have proven to be effective. Do you remember a time that you had a gut feeling about something and it turned out to be accurate? Maybe you knew you shouldn't do something but did not listen to yourself and ended up causing a mess. Whatever it was, sit down with your journal and write about it.

What do you remember about that moment? Was it a vision you had? A scent? Write about the clairsense in as much detail as you can. Don't leave anything out. The thoughts you had and the way you reacted in this instance are both important. Even what you were wearing when this happened and who you were with is relevant.

Taking time to recognize every detail will help you become more aware. For example, if you notice that your bottom lip gets numb when you have a clairvoyant vision, that's an indicator. Documenting each experience will help you identify the difference between clairsense moments and mundane ones.

TRY THIS
Meditation

A tried and true method for developing your clairsenses is through meditation. When you stop your mind from racing, you are able to really pay attention to the world around you. For the next couple of days, take fifteen minutes and be still. What senses are accentuated during this time? If sounds stand out, start focusing on them. If something pops up in your mind's eye, take notice. You may even smell, feel, or taste something during these meditations. Discern whether or not there is a message in what you are sensing.

Finding control over your mind will lead to controlling your extra sensory experiences. You will find that eventually the process becomes natural. Once you've reached this state, you'll be open to all the clairsense messages that are trying to come through.

Suggested Reading

Psychic Witch: A Metaphysical Guide to Meditation, Magick, and Manifestation by Mat Auryn. Llewellyn Publications, 2020.

Llewellyn's Little Book of Psychic Development by Melanie Barnum. Llewellyn Publications, 2017.

3
There Is No Wrong Way To Witch

No matter who you are, there are a number of rules we all have no choice but to submit to. Whether they are laws of nature or a nation, no one is free of certain restrictions like gravity, death, or taxes. There are three main places where a majority of these limitations are imposed upon us. Universal laws are unavoidable; this includes things like the laws of relativity, gestation, vibration, polarity, and so on. Then there are the laws of a nation. You *could* break these rules, but they tend to carry serious consequences like the death penalty or life in prison for committing murder. Finally, there are the laws of religion.

Religious rules aren't a necessity. None of us are required to follow a religion, and yet according to the World Factbook by the Central Intelligence Agency of the United States, more than half of the world's population subscribes to one of the three Abrahamic religions. In strong contrast to this statistic, a third of us follow one of fifteen different world religions. Finally, less than fourteen percent of the world is free of religious belief in general. Looking at these facts makes it clear that spirituality is a vital part of our human existence for the vast majority of people. But can we have spirituality without laws? Is it imperative to maintain a structure in order to connect to the Source?

Witchcraft is not technically a religion. While many practitioners view it as such, it is important to point out that there is a dichotomy of interfaith Witches. From Christian Witches to Atheist ones, the diversity of religion attached to Witchcraft is vast and as unique as each individual practicing it. Many people throughout history have attempted to define this practice of magickal skills and abilities. In the past, "Wicca" and "Witchcraft" were used interchangeably, but now more than ever before the issue is that the definition tends to vary from culture to culture. What's more, every Witch has their own explanation of the practice. My definition is that Witchcraft is the pursuit of wisdom. In other words, I seek knowledge. How does my energy interact with the moon, the seasons, red jasper, or amethyst? I endeavor to understand my own mind and its ability to pick up on the transmissions it receives from the past, present, and future. My goal as a Witch is to get in sync with the vibration of everything I share this physical existence with while attempting to bend it to my will as needed. Witchcraft is an infinite journey of learning.

My Story: Magic Bells Aren't Magick

Once I was a boy sitting in a church pew, calling forth all the patience a child could possibly muster. I sat as still as I could, fidgeting and kicking the kneelers, doing my best to reel it in each time the back of my arm was discreetly pinched as a reminder. Music began to play and everyone stood up. A calm would wash over me as the priest walked in and took his place at the altar.

I thought church was magical, that it really was angels ringing the bells as the robed man up front lifted the body of Christ to the heavens. Even after learning that magic bells aren't magick, I believed. With the knowledge that the blood of Christ wasn't truly transformed from wine, I held onto faith. I thought my sins were forgiven each time I told my darkest secrets.

That was life every Sunday. Believing that the Catholic Church was the real deal, that it was the only true path. I knew every word to the mass. I'd sit, stand, and kneel repeating each word as it came out of the priest's mouth. I longed for the day that I could become an altar boy, I wanted to be close to God.

In second grade, I went to Catholic school. The teachers hated me. They'd say, "He can't sit still in class, but he's so well behaved in mass." On career day they asked us to draw for them what we wanted to be when we grew up. Some of the other kids wanted to work in construction like their dads, others figured they would be lawyers or doctors. Me, I was going to become a priest.

By twelve years old I'd wake up every Sunday and walk to the local church. Eventually, puberty set in and I started wishing that grown men would stop their cars and offer a proposition as I walked to church. This became a problem, noticing handsome men. I paid less attention to the mass and more attention to the hot dads in attendance.

Already sexually active, I was fooling around or attempting to do so with all my male friends. Lusting after every man I saw, my libido was in overdrive, which led to bad choices. I would go into confession and attempt to seduce the priest. Genuine in my desire, I tried to tempt the priest into breaking his vow of celibacy. Inevitably, this behavior blew up in my face. One priest caught on to what I was doing. He told me not to come back into confession with those sorts of stories.

The next week, that same priest gave his sermon about the sin of homosexuality. He might as well have had his hand on my shoulder saying, "This is an example of what not to be." At that moment it all sunk in. I was gay and not welcome in the church. This sermon was the cake topper. It seemed that all of a sudden, even God thought I was wrong for being the person he created. My faith was broken; I was abandoned for loving men. I stopped going to church.

Summer ended and I held onto my secret for fear of everyone's reaction. In seventh grade, I thought I had a crush on a girl but as the school year started, I realized I just really liked her hair. It was long, pencil straight, and red. She wore flowy skirts made of thin material and hung out with the goth kids.

In eighth grade, I found out we walked the same path to school. Both of us eager to find someone to walk with, I decided to offer my companionship. I was shocked when she said yes. We spent the first quarter of the year developing a friendship. By the time it got too cold to walk, we were well on our way to being friends. We'd sneak cigarettes and hang out after school. She was the first person I ever told I was gay. She accepted it without a second thought.

She told me secrets too: she and her mom were Witches, and her boyfriend had already graduated high school. I was introduced to a lot in our friendship. We'd sit in her room listening to Tori Amos while reading Silver RavenWolf. On the floor of her bedroom, the idea of God transformed into gods and goddesses. The Father, Son, and Holy Ghost became Earth, Fire, Air, and Water. And "don't be gay" was replaced with "harm none and do what ye will."

Considering myself no longer abandoned, my fire-haired Witch stood up for me when I kicked the closet door down, announcing to the world that I was gay. When I had troubles at home, she talked her mom into taking me in for a little while. Eventually I moved away, failing to keep my promise of staying in touch. Holding on to my enlightenment, I carried a new sense of strength with me. Believing myself to be a Witch, I was unaware that I had only learned about Wicca.

If I Had Known

I was a teen when I first laid eyes on *To Ride a Silver Broomstick*. The fact is that even though her books were about Wicca, what I learned from Silver RavenWolf set the tone for everything that came after. It gave me a knowledge base that helped me grow at my own pace into what I am now.

Silver RavenWolf paved the way for a lot of my generation's occult writers. She was able to reach people like me and my contemporaries long before we had websites like Patheos. Silver RavenWolf changed my life just as much as my friend in the long, flowy skirts did. But instead of freeing myself of religion as I had thought, instead it turned out that I forsook one system of beliefs for another. If I had known as a teen that to be a Witch did not require following rules, I may have developed as a practitioner a bit quicker.

As I've matured, I've grown to understand that rules don't serve me that well. What makes me a Witch is not my ability to follow certain steps in the creation of magick. I am a Witch because I understand how energy flows through me. I understand that energy doesn't flow through everyone the same way. And I am much more aware these days that a strong practice is developed by understanding magick from multiple angles.

Over time I have learned that if something resonates with me, I should probably use it. For instance, cascarilla is commonly known for its origins in Santería. I have no ties to Cuba or the continent of Africa, yet I find that powdered egg shells work well for me when I am using protection magick, something that I came into it naturally. I listened with my claircognizance and trusted what I knew. It wasn't until after I had been using egg shells in my work that I learned it was something other people did.

What took me a long time to figure out was that no matter what, magick doesn't have rules—people have rules. People want to control situations as best they can; they want to run the show. This is a form of gatekeeping, a common issue in the Witchcraft community when other Witches try to enforce rules that don't actually exist. These Witches stand at a hypothetical gate and hold it shut against practitioners who won't fall in line with what these people believe to be the only way to do things.

What Makes a Witch

To be a Witch is to harness the energy, spirit, or power from the world around you. This means a practitioner will use stones, feathers, dead animals, herbs, celestial events, and more to empower their magickal workings. The title "Witch" is one that only we can place upon ourselves. We are all magickal regardless of our labels. Unless you choose to call ourselves one, you are not a Witch. We could use tarot and light candles, see ghosts and be clairvoyant too, all while not being a Witch. Lots of people do these things and they aren't Witches because they don't see themselves as one.

On the other side of the coin, a person could be doing none of those things and they might fully identify as a Witch. In this case, they most definitely are and here is why. The first thing that makes a Witch a Witch is an innate sense that they are one. Before I knew that I could even be a Witch I felt a stirring of magick within me. I would liken this to gender identity. A trans person identifies as trans before they begin their transition. They know before anyone else who they really are. A person could know their true gender for years before they are able to finally live a life as such. In the same way, a person's identity as a Witch emerges long before their practice is underway. Secondly, a Witch is a Witch because they say so. Being a Witch doesn't mean you are dancing in the moonlight on every full moon. It doesn't mean you have to have an altar or that you collect herbs. Being a Witch is who you are, not what you look like or how you behave.

What we see on the big and small screens of media are hyperfantastic depictions of Witches. On this show they might be able to stop time, in that movie they can levitate. These special powers bestowed upon Witches in television and movies supersede physics. They are obviously unattainable. Although these powers are often exaggerations of actual practices, they only hold value in terms of entertainment and nothing else.

Real Witches aren't out there fighting demons and moving things with their minds. They aren't pyrokinetic or in league with the devil. Real Witches are people like you and me. They are going to work every day, paying bills, and often struggling to make ends meet. There are people who would have you believe they can do these otherworldly things. More often than not these people have some form of mental instability.

A Witch is a person actively trying to understand the world around them. They may want to find a better flow with the energy in their surroundings or attempt to understand themselves in order to heal. What makes a Witch is the path of discovery; Witches seek knowledge above all things. Then, if they choose, Witches can use this knowledge to manipulate the world they live in.

JOURNAL PROMPT
What Makes You a Witch?

In your journal, list the things that you identify as Witchy in your life. Is your love for candles deeper than the scent they provide when you light them? Do you give gratitude for everything? Are you drawn to the ocean or other bodies of water?

For this writing exercise, examine your connection to the word Witch and how it affects your connection to your environment. If the flicker of a candle flame mesmerizes you explain why that maintains your connection to Witchcraft. If you find your most magickal moments to be when you wake up at three a.m. for no reason, describe in your journal why you feel that way.

Taking the time to write out what connects you to Witchcraft will serve as a reminder later if you start to doubt yourself. Rereading the list with your explanations is a great way to anchor yourself to your own identity of being a Witch. In a world where others may try to control the narrative on what being a Witch is all about, having a firm understanding of *your* definition of your practice is a sure fire way to remain grounded in your belief system.

Not All Witches Are Wiccan

The difference between Wicca and Witchcraft is something I wish I had understood from the very beginning. There are a lot of differences between the two, for instance that not all Wiccans identify as Witches. Wicca is a religion created by Gerald Gardner in the 1950s; as religions go, Wicca is pretty young. It is built around a lot of Pagan and nature-based ideas. Wiccans honor a God and a Goddess as well as nature. There are rituals and rites in Wicca, but spells are not a requirement.

Witchcraft doesn't fit neatly into a little box; rather, it falls into a large encompassing ring with several off-shoot practices. Witchcraft isn't a religion in and of itself although many practitioners view it as such. For others it is more than religion: it is a practice, a skill that takes exercise to perfect. Witches can be Christian, Jewish, Wiccan, or any other religion. They often combine several belief systems into a practice that works for them personally. Religion is not a prerequisite for being a Witch in any way.

It is common to find covens of Witches who share the role of leader. Often this role rotates through each initiate, allowing everyone to gain experience and to play an active role. Setting a system up in this way keeps everyone on an equal playing field while creating a dynamic experience for all involved.

Witchcraft is a journey. Picture yourself in the woods at night. There is a fork in the road and more than one way into the forest presents itself for you. This is the way Witchcraft works. You can choose one path and walk into an experience that leads into developing your psychic abilities. Conversely you could take another path and learn all about the Greek pantheon, honoring only those deities. Additionally there are paths that lead to both and others that lead to neither.

We call Witchcraft the path of the wise because it is a practice of constant learning. No one reaches a point in magick where they can say, "Okay, that's it. I've learned all I need to know." Because magick is diverse, there is no end to what a person can learn if they continue to endeavor to do so.

When I was just starting out, no one was there to tell me that I had options. Everyone at the time seemed to think that there was only one way—theirs. This is not the case. What may be good for the goose is not good for me. In the beginning, I lacked the guidance I needed to identify what worked for me and what did not. It takes trial and error to really find your footing in the magickal world.

After falling from grace and rebelling against dogma; as a younger teen I was not prepared to be told magick can only be performed a certain way. Back in the day, I was taught that cursing was wrong, that anything I put into the world would come back to me. The three-fold law is a common thing in the Wiccan religion, whereas in the Satanic church they teach you that if a man smites you, you smite him back, which is more along the lines of how I see the world. While I also don't agree with all the principles of the Satanists, I see just as much value in some of their teachings as I do in all other religions.

Witchcraft is an ancient practice of magick that has gone through all kinds of evolutions throughout history. No one today can truly say with certainty what a bunch of people in the past were doing or why they were doing it. At best, we can only make guesses.

Because there are so many paths to walk in the Witching world, it is important to explore as many of them as you feel drawn to. Not all Witches need a coven; some thrive in their own solitary practices, and other Witches identify themselves through their community relationships. All of these paths are valid. As a new Witch, it is a great idea to try multiple things until you find the right fit for you. You wouldn't just buy the first pair of shoes you see in a store, would you? You would try on a couple pairs and make sure the colors, design, and fit were right for you. Finding your way in your magickal practice is going to be a lifelong adventure, it is possible you will develop new ideas that change your mind from how you felt originally. Try on as many of those ideas as you believe is necessary. And to extend the analogy, if at some point you need a new pair of shoes, don't be afraid to throw out the old pair. Sometimes we outgrow things in our lives. Getting rid of the worn out, tattered ideas that don't fit us anymore isn't a crime, it is evolution.

TRY THIS
Join Communities

Facebook, Twitter, Instagram, and Reddit are all rich with communities of Witches. There are groups for learning and places where you can share ideas. Online communities are the ripest ground for you to harvest your identity as a Witch.

Seek out groups of Witches that resonate with you. Find a social group that will allow you to ask questions and learn. By joining the communities in these platforms, you are going to be afforded the opportunity to develop a feel for what you do and don't believe. The best part is that these places are all virtual so you don't have to leave the house to find them and you can maintain your anonymity as long as you like. The other perfect aspect of joining the community in this way is that if you find that a group doesn't really work for you, you can simply cut ties.

Making Witch friends is going to help you grow. People in these groups are at all different levels and places in their journey. Some may end up guiding you, and eventually you may find that you end up guiding some of them as well.

If You Decide to Work with Deities

Not all Witches work with deities. Because there are so many options for a Witch's practice, it is common to find Witches who disagree with the idea of gods and goddesses just as often as you will find those who agree with the practice. While some Witches work with the elements and others work with energy there are still plenty that work with deity, energy, and the elements. This is what's right for them. Just like I wouldn't want to be told to practice a certain way, it is likely these Witches like to do things their way as well.

I chose to work with a deity from a non-religious point of view. The way I see my connection is much more symbiotic than one of worship.

When I started taking Witchcraft seriously, I found Hekate. For me Hekate is the oldest idea of divinity that I could relate to. Because her name means so much and has been around for so long, there is power in the idea of her. The thing I fell in love with about Hekate is the ability to tap into specific aspects of her by using her epithets. When I call upon a specific aspect of the Goddess, I am still calling out to Hekate herself. The difference is that when I use an epithet I am focusing my energy into this particular thing. All of this is really just my access point to the Source itself; for me Hekate is an egregore. By working with her I am narrowing down exactly what I am after and specifying the pathway that gets me there.

You could spend time learning about every deity known to humanity. You could explore to your heart's content. Maybe you'll find something that works for you. But if you never find a deity that's okay too. There are lots of different kinds of Witches. At the end of the day, the manner in which any one of us taps into the Source isn't important—what is important is that it works. Finding deities is fine; they don't have to belong to the same pantheon or anything, but be sure you dive deep into learning about them. If those deities will be your access point to the Source the way that Hekate is mine, then you will want to understand the role they have played throughout history.

There are several reasons you'll want to understand the deities you work with, the main one being that they are not your property. Deities have been around for a long time. Some of the common gods and goddesses found in the Pagan community are older than the bible itself. Knowing where these deities come from, how they were worshiped, and what they stand for is important in a lot of ways.

Not all Witches agree with me on this, but I believe that humans created deities. I don't think they did this on purpose to control each other. I also believe that there was already something there that the deities were created out of, the Source. What I believe is people spent a lot of time worshiping these entities. There has been a lot of energy poured into the idea of gods such as Odin and Ganesha. When that energy has gone into the same idea for centuries, it literally creates an entity of that deity. In other words, all deities are an extension of the Source. Through our belief and worship of them they become their own separate entities though. They remain individuals and continue to exist independent of people, but it is people who first create them. That said, going to the goddess of wisdom and asking her to assist you with a love spell probably won't get you as far as going to a goddess of love and romance will.

When we learn about a deity, we are learning about the culture that built them. If we take this cultural truth and then pervert it in order to fit our needs, we are being disrespectful. The horrible part is that we aren't just disrespecting the culture that we are basically appropriating, but we are also disrespecting the deity as well.

You aren't wrong for being drawn to the Hindu pantheon even though you're a suburban Caucasian who's never left the town you were born in. If you have done your research, learned all that you can, and honor those deities with respect, then you're doing all the right things. No one can say why you're drawn to a practice. You might not even know why at first. Now, it is your responsibility to look into it, though. Maybe it's your past life coming through, or maybe that pantheon sees your valor. Either way, you took the first step and answered their call. Don't let another person cause you to shy away from this connection.

JOURNAL PROMPT
Why God, Why?

If you are working with a deity, take the time to identify why you were drawn to them. Write out all the things that led you to finding this particular entity. Explore whether or not they have been present in your life before you knew about them. Have you always been a traveler or a thief only to find that you are drawn to Hermes later in life?

When we take the time to connect to the reason we resonate with a deity, it becomes easier to communicate with them. Write out all the things you know about the god or goddess you work with. Then draw the connection to how those things relate to you. Once you've done this, you will have a record of your relationship that will create a tighter bond to your deity in the long run.

Appropriation

It is common these days for people to worry about cultural appropriation. This is when a person from one culture adopts elements from another culture. This is frowned upon in the Witching world; people fail to realize that smudging is an indigenous practice and that palo santo wood should be harvested in particular and sacred ways. In other words, people start using practices they don't understand and throw around terms as if they were born into that practice, when really, it's just something they felt an affinity for and incorporated. Sometimes, though, you will have an idea for a tool you can use and then later learn it is part of another culture's practice, which does not constitute cultural appropriation. What matters is the intention.

Cultures are appropriated all the time. It was only recently that anyone other than scientists used the term. One only needs to open a fashion magazine or watch a music video to see this behavior in action. Pop stars pick and choose accessories that have religious meanings to practicing Hindus just to look cute. Models walk the runway in headdresses despite the fact that they are neither in a ceremony or a war, never mind that they aren't the male leader of a tribe. These are examples of inappropriate appropriation.

As the modern world has developed, so has the Witch. "Eclectic" is one of the most common terms a Witch uses when describing themselves. This is because we have access to information. Since learning is key to the development of a Witch it's no wonder that these days we mix kitchen magick with Hoodoo, that we read tarot, runes, tea leaves, and cast lots. By our nature, we are on an everlasting mission to know more, to understand how things work on a spiritual level. So why wouldn't we seek out knowledge outside of our culture?

We live in a world that is connected in all sorts of ways. We network with people we've never met in the flesh. We carry an infinite library of resources in our pockets, and there is no limit to the information at our fingertips. Considering the technological advantages we have, it is safe to say that not understanding a practice is just plain lazy these days. For example, there is no issue with performing a smoke cleanse as long as you have taken the time to learn why you would use sage to do it and why sage is considered sacred to some indigenous peoples. I personally prefer bay leaves for this act because it resonates with my cultural upbringing as an American with grandparents who moved here from Sicily. Beyond that, the deity I work with is closely associated with the plant.

It doesn't matter where a particular practice originated as long as you understand its context before making it your own. Smoke has been used in many cultures to cleanse a person or a space, so ask yourself why you think sage or palo santo in particular are right for you to use. If your answer isn't convincing, perhaps it is time to change your practice up.

TRY THIS
Tread Respectfully

Which plants are important to your culture or even your environment? Take the time to learn if any of these plants correspond with purification, healing, or protection. A Witch's natural resources should be their go-to materials.

The place you live is no accident, neither is how you were raised. These things are already attuned to your vibration, and they exist with you in your space. Using the naturally growing plants around you is going to have a lot more power for you personally than the wood from a tree that grows in Central America.

Witches can make their own smoking sticks. Your environment is full of usable plants that can be dried and burnt in order to cleanse your surroundings. After identifying a few plants that grow near you, go out and harvest them (although be sure not to break any laws in doing so.) Wrap your plants in twine and hang them to dry for a few days. Once they are dry, they are ready to burn.

Magick is about intention more than anything else, so before you burn your bundle, spend some time placing your intention into it. Are you cleansing your space? Setting a ward? Once you know what you are doing and why you are doing it, you have developed your own practice that will feel right to you.

TRY THIS
Using Other Cultures

If you really resonate with the idea of sage and palo santo, learn how it is harvested in the right way. Start researching where you can buy it from people who are doing this correctly. Additionally, learn all you can about the culture these smoke practices come from. It is important to understand why each plant is used in order to best integrate it into your practice.

Your Practice Is Yours

Witchcraft doesn't have to be dogmatic. Lots of traditions will tell you, "You can't do this." Or, "You can only do that." They will push ideas like the three-fold laws or the idea that only women can be Witches. If those ideas don't feel right to you, then they aren't. Of course at some point we get what we give, but is what we receive in return going to be three times as good or bad as your deed? Not likely. And, males can be Witches too; many men can attest to this, myself included. Being a man in the Craft doesn't mean we don't hold equal space for women or non-gender-conforming people. I am a dyed-in-the-wool feminist and believe in equality across the board for all people.

I searched for years to find the right fit for my beliefs. I would be foolish to tell you or anyone that my way is the right way. My way works for me because it resonates for me. I tried Christianity, manifesting through the Law of Attractions, a little Hinduism, and even a few attempts at petitioning demons.

Your practice doesn't have to look like anyone else's. Just because Karen from the coven likes to open her circles with the Lesser Pentagram Banishing Ritual doesn't mean you have to. How you open your circles is for you to say. You set the rules. I believe in your right to make that decision for yourself.

Suggested Reading

Weave the Liminal by Laura Tempest Zakroff. Llewellyn Publications, 2019.

Transformative Witchcraft: The Greater Mysteries by Jason Mankey. Llewellyn Publications, 2019.

Witchery: Embrace the Witch Within by Juliet Diaz. Hay House, 2019.

True Magic: Unleashing Your Inner Witch by Cyndi Brannen. Moon Books, 2019.

4
Protect Yourself

Protection magick can be a powerful ally when you need it. The sheer force of will to protect oneself is an innate trait in every one of us. The example of a mother lifting a car off of her child comes to mind. When our safety or the safety of a loved one is at stake we can become superhuman. A Witch is no different. If the fact that we have a list of tools from herbs to stones and incantations with the specific purpose of protection isn't evidence enough, consider the *PMG*. The *Papyri Graecae Magicae*, otherwise known as the *Greek Magical Papyri* is one of the oldest collections of spells in the world. Within this text you can find workings to call a supernatural assistant to you, secure the affection of another, and you can find spells which are meant to help you protect yourself.

Safety is at the forefront of most magickal practices. It is why we cast a circle and purify a space. Protection is how we take control when we access powers greater than ourselves. We set boundaries with spirits and humans alike in our efforts to ward off any negativity in our lives. In doing so, we stand firm in the fact that we are indeed a force in our own right. Witches are not only imbued with the power of the Source, nature, and the gods and goddesses but also with the knowledge and wisdom to put that power into motion.

Banishing, binding, warding, and creating amulets are just a few ways a Witch can protect themselves. There is no limit to the application of self-defense that magick provides. Safeguarding is essential in the Witching world not only in regard to the practitioner but also for those around them. While security is necessary from a magickal point of view, it is also often practical for mundane things in life as well.

> **A Caveat:** First and foremost, if you believe you or someone you care about is in a dangerous situation, seek help. Abuse is a very real thing and magick should not be your first course of action. Magick is unfortunately not a cure-all, and very serious problems often need mundane action to be resolved. It is highly important that we as Witches use our power of discernment to identify when a more mundane approach is in order.

My Story: Block My Abuser

One thing has repeatedly happened to me throughout my existence: Witches find their way into my life. In Pennsylvania, it was my high school friend, the one who really introduced me to my path. I was worried at first that I'd never find another Witch when I moved away. Not long after living in Oklahoma, I was proven wrong.

At the time, I was deep inside an abusive experience with my caretaker. This relationship encompassed several levels of abuse from physical to emotional to mental. The abuser suffered from a lack of confidence and extreme insecurities that I seemed to trigger on a regular basis. They were in control of the situation and there was nothing I could do to free myself. Reaching out for help from the authorities was useless. Even the person who should have been my protector allowed this tyrant to take their pain and anger out on me.

In this part of my life, I was constantly unsure of my safety. If I didn't eat all my greens at dinner or I arrived home three minutes late from school, I faced the chance that fists would fly at my face. The word "faggot" was used more often than my own name. I was convinced I was ugly and stupid—I was told so every day. When I was beaten for minor things, I was told that my nose was so big, it was an easy target. It was common for me to taste my own blood running down the back of my throat as I walked to my room, crying after an encounter.

I spent three years in this hell as the abuse grew more and more violent. I was a literal punching bag for a broken woman who saw that she was getting away with taking her pain out on a child. I attempted all the mundane fixes. Child Protective Services failed me three times in two different states. Eventually I had to accept that this was my burden to carry.

Isolated from the world in the outskirts of a town without a bus system for their high school, I was alone. The only escape available could be found between 8 a.m. and 3 p.m., while I attended class. I made friends easily and the friends I made wanted to help me out of my situation. I received varied forms of assistance from advice to escape routes. But none of that ever actually worked. It wasn't until a Witch stepped in to assist that I saw true results.

I was arrested for being a runaway although I did not run away. The sadist ruling over my life threatened me one morning as I was getting ready for school. "If you come home tonight, I'm going to kill you." I was told, "Don't come home." Friends jumped into action. One assured me it would be okay to sleep at his house. I ended up sleeping in a closet hidden away from his parents. The next three nights, another friend took me in whose parents were fully aware of my situation. The rule was that I couldn't stay past Monday morning.

That weekend, I visited another friend from school who identified herself as a Witch to me. She said she wanted to give me a gift. As we talked, she pulled out a little black sack. She told me to hold it. We walked out to her mother's garden and she began to pick herbs as I told her, "I just don't want to get beaten up anymore." I told her I wanted to block my abuser from any further attacks.

We went inside and sat on the floor in her room. She had me open the bag. She placed intentions into the herbs and lit a candle, asked me to envision my life free of abuse, to picture what that would look like. I did as instructed. When the candle burned out, she pulled a piece of wax dripping from the holder. She asked for my hand and pricked my finger with my permission. We took the resulting blood and rubbed it all over the candle wax. After this, she sealed the bag. I was meant to wear it at all times and to never open it.

I left the Witch's house feeling a true sense of safety. I went home on Monday after school. My caretakers told me to wait outside while they called the cops to come arrest me. As I was arrested, my custodians mentioned that they would pick me up when they got around to it. I had already told the officer what really happened. A smile spread across my face when the policeman turned to them and said, "If you aren't there in twenty minutes, I'll be back to arrest you for abandonment of a minor." The mojo bag was already working.

I was fifteen at the time and dealing with severe emotional damage. I made a mistake when we first moved to Oklahoma. This was one of those mistakes that changes your life forever. A week after my arrest that blunder came to light. Thankfully this was the sort of error that ended up having me admitted into a behavioral health treatment center. Not only did my faux pas liberate me from the abuse, but it also delivered much needed psychological help for an issue that had been hiding in the shadows for a decade.

I never went back to my abuser after that. The magick performed to protect me worked. I stopped getting beaten up, received the mental health care that I desperately needed, and was able to heal before the mistake I made became a habit. Not only was I protected from my abuser but I was also protected from myself. Things were not rainbows and unicorns afterward. I became a high school dropout, lost all my friends in Oklahoma, and eventually became a homeless teen. Regardless of any issues that developed after the protection spell did its job, I am grateful for the Witch and her magick that day. Because of her, I was released from a three-year residency in a hell designed to break my spirit. I emerged not completely broken.

If I Had Known

If we take a look at the mundane world around us, it is easy to see the myriad ways in which we are able to protect ourselves.

We have weapons, fences, camera and alarm systems, and even physical self-defense, which are all things you can do or use to safeguard yourself from danger. Beyond that, it's possible to find personal safety devices at work such as safety glasses, gloves, ear plugs, and much more. There is no end to the ways in which we are able to maintain our own well-being. If I had known that there was a magickal route to defending myself from abuse as a child, it is possible that I could have beaten my abuser to the punch long before landing myself in a mental health facility.

There is a plethora of ways to use magick as a means to protect yourself. Apotropaic magick such as talismans and wards around your home can be used as a first defense. Banishing and binding spells are excellent counterattacks as well. Stones can be used to absorb the negative energy around you. And herbs are often combined or used alone in smoke cleansings meant to push out forces that are oppressing us in some way. Protection spells are plentiful and are often quite powerful when used in combination with real-world solutions. There are other not so obvious forms of protection as well, such as swaying someone's behavior to be more kind. It's even possible to completely cut a person from your life with other types of spells.

Having a firm understanding of the limits of magick is vital when figuring out how best to protect yourself. For instance, it would be foolish to assume that magick could make us bulletproof. In that same vein, it would not be ideal to expect protection magick to completely block any sort of legal ramifications which are rightfully due.

Protection spells don't always work the way you expect them to. Sometimes a protection spell could put you into a position where you are protected by a circumstance. For instance, you may have an abusive spouse. To protect yourself from them you might do a spell, a week later they end up going to jail for years because of tax evasion. While your intention was not explicitly for them to be put in jail, they cannot harm you because they've been locked up. What's more, you would now have the space needed in order to truly leave them before they are released.

One important thing to remember about protective magick is that it is dynamic: it can be worked in a pinch during an emergency or it can be planned. Results may vary, but typically the intention in these situations is often passionate and therefore holds a great deal of power for that reason alone. You could do this work with big extravagant rituals and spells or find a beautiful piece of obsidian and simply just begin wearing it with not much effort placed in the act. Either way, the defense is in place. When planning out your spells and rituals, you will find that there are ideal times to do these sorts of things. Knowing when those powerful moments are will certainly help to add strength to your intentions.

Magickal Timing for Protection

In and of itself, the moon is a magickal tool—it has an energy and a vibration that allows us to tap into specific things at specific times. In addition, each day of the week has magickal attributes, as do astrological signs. Not only can you plan your protection work in order to empower it for optimal efficiency, you have several options to do so. This allows for a certain level of flexibility in your planning. None of this timing is hard and fast; if timing doesn't resonate with you, don't worry about it. Especially when it comes to protection magick, it should resonate with you and your intentions more than anything else.

Lunar Phases

Lunar phases play a role in magick because just like every one of us, magick has a cycle. That cycle can best be seen in correlation to the moon. Many Witches coordinate their spells and rituals to the moon's phases. In the case of protection magick, it is the waning moon that is most empowering.

The waning moon takes place from the time that the full moon ends until the dark moon begins; it is when the moon starts to look like it is going away. Protection magick, banishing rituals, and bindings to prevent continuing harm are all about the removal of something in our lives. Whether we are ridding ourselves of an abuser or avoiding a speeding ticket, the general sense of the working is sending away an obstacle. The association is clear—a waning moon appears to be losing its volume. As the moon appears to decrease, so do the issues at hand.

Days of the Week

Days of the week hold power, and each is connected to a specific planet. These planets correspond to deities from the Greek, Roman, and Norse pantheons and are said to hold the same rule over things that relate to its respective god or goddess. The sun and moon are very clearly associated with Sunday and Monday. Tuesday, however, is connected to Mars. The day receives its name from the Norse god Tiw or Tyr. This was a god of war, which ties him to the Greek Ares and the Roman Mars.

Since these three gods were all rulers of war, Tuesday is a powerful day regarding warlike things. What we all know about war is that it involves a lot of setting boundaries and defending things—in other words, protection. If you are planning work meant to safeguard you in some way, a Tuesday is a perfect choice to perform it.

Time of Day
In addition to the days of the week, the hours also hold a great deal of magickal energy. The full energy of the sun is at its peak at midday, which means that working with the sun at noon each day can greatly increase your spells' potency. Everything is revealed at noon—shadows are at their smallest. And as it turns out, this is also the best time of day to perform protection magick.

Astrological Signs
Astrological signs can be used for other reasons beyond our personality traits and the houses and planets that are positioned within them in our natal charts. They can also add a great deal of kick to our spells. The signs of the zodiac and planets remain in a constant rotation around us. They change not only in monthly increments but also in daily ones as well. When someone asks you what your sign is, you typically answer with your sun sign. This is the position of the sun on the day you were born. What many people don't know is that you also have a moon sign and many others.

The positions of both the sun and the moon can play a role in your personality. Additionally, these same factors can affect the power of your magickal workings. Knowing which sign the sun is in helps when planning out rituals and spells because each sign carries with it their own set of strengths and weaknesses. The same holds true for the moon. There are two in particular that correspond with protection magick: Scorpio and Aries are both ruled by Mars and thus have some of its warlike aspects.

Moon and Sign Placement

Being a water sign, Scorpio can be dynamic—water tends to flow and ebb. Considering this fact, how it reacts to the lunar phase is important in magick. Self-defense, protection, and banishing spells work best for this sign during a waning moon.

Aries, on the other hand, is a fire sign. Fire burns until it consumes all there is to envelop. It can be a lot less dynamic but is still equally as strong. With Aries, the phase of the moon does not affect its effect on our magick. This means that no matter the moon's current phase, as long as it is in Aries, it's a good time for protection magick.

Sun Placement

Though the moon is a great celestial being to draw magick from, we should never fail to acknowledge the power of the sun. After all, the sun is a force that energizes the world around us. It helps things grow and is commonly considered to deliver a sense of happiness. As far as zodiac signs are concerned, the sun remains in a sign for about thirty days. This means that twice a year you'll have thirty solid days to work protection magick. The sun in Aries (March 20 to April 21) or Scorpio (October 23 to November 22) are both good times to draw on the power of the sun for protection magick.

There is a lot of complicated information to consume in regard to using timing and planetary placements in magick. If it seems confusing to you, that's okay—when it comes to protection, go with what feels right. Just because there are times, days, signs, and lunar phases that work well for the endeavor, it doesn't mean those are the *only* times you can do the magick. If you need protection, the right time is right away.

TRY THIS
Doorway Protection

Once you have chosen your perfect timing try this simple spell to protect the doorway of your home or even just a bedroom.

What You'll Need
- Salt
- A bowl

The Process

Pour the salt into the bowl. Sit with the salt at the special time you have identified for protection magick. In your mind, recall the reasons this moment is special for you as it relates to protection. Visualize the energy of this timing being pulled into the bowl of salt. Once you have drawn the magickal energy of this timing into the salt, sprinkle it along the floor of your door frame. As you sprinkle, place the intentions of protection into it. Know that this time you have chosen is imbued into each granule. As the salt scatters on the floor, envision a barrier rising to encompass the doorway.

Set the bowl of salt beside the door. Reapply any time you sweep or vacuum the area of the doorway. You can also reapply the protection salt anytime you feel you need a little added protection.

Wards

A few wards you may be aware of are based on superstitions and religious beliefs. Have you ever seen those decorations (typically made of glass) that look like blue circles that have a smaller white one and a black dot in the center? These are called *nazar* and are wards against the Evil Eye. This type of magick is called apotropaic magick; it is meant to ward off evil or bad luck. Many cultures throughout the world have similar items, gestures, or words for this purpose. Sometimes it's a fist with the pinky and index finger extended, in Italy it is a red horn that somewhat resembles a pepper. The Pennsylvania Dutch are known for the huge wards called hex signs painted on their barns. While the hex signs have several different uses, many are meant to protect and ward off danger.

In my car I have talismans that hang on my rearview mirror. They are special charms that mean something to me and stay in my vehicle. All the items had purpose before they were made into wards; when I was able to identify how they worked for protection, I gave them a new job. Some are traditional family practices handed down through culture and others were intuitive; I found the objects and knew they were meant to protect me. I've taken the time to empower them to protect me while I'm driving, which makes them wards because these objects are meant to guard me in my travels. They protect me from things like collisions and the deer that love to run out in front of my car when I'm driving to work in the fall.

Creating the ward can be simple enough. It is important to point out that when identifying or creating wards, it takes intention to really give them power. You could walk into a store and see a candle labeled as "protection," buy it, take it home, and light it. That's great, but it isn't likely to do a whole lot for you if you stop there.

Magick works based on the work you put into it. Lighting a candle labeled "protection" is no different than lighting an ordinary candle bought at the corner store. All it's going to do is make a pretty flickering light and maybe a nice scent. Unless you've put intentions into the protection candle, it is basically mundane.

Using wards takes energy. The intention put into your ward is what activates it. When I started down the path of Witchcraft, I was unaware of the effects of intentions for years. I figured I could light my candles and say some words and they would do their job, but that's not the way this works. When setting a ward now, I know that I have to put my energy into the protection. I need to identify exactly what I am protecting myself against. In order to get the best results out of this and any magick, I need to match it to my vibration.

Wards can be dynamic in that they take on several different forms. Some simple wards can be placed around your house. One in particular that I've learned of involves railroad spikes, red string and your urine. Others are the more well-known items like the hamsa or the nazar mentioned earlier. An obsidian necklace worn daily that absorbs negativity is an excellent example of one as well. Once you've set the intention and charged the jewelry with your vibration, you've created something powerful—and it looks nice too. Now when you wear the necklace, the ward is on autopilot, protecting you as you go through your day.

TRY THIS
Making a Protection Talisman

This is a process for making an item that can be used to protect you. This would be something you would carry with you all the time.

What You'll Need

- A talisman—it could be anything from a piece of jewelry to a feather you've found on the ground.

- Bay leaves

- Dragon's blood resin

- Charcoal tab

- A fire-safe dish

The Process

First, cleanse the item. Break up the bay leaves and grind the dragon's blood resin. Combine the two into a mixture. In your fire-safe dish, light the charcoal and then sprinkle your mixture onto it. The mixture will create a smoke for you to pass your talisman through.

If you don't have access to the items above, tap water works in a pinch.

When passing your talisman through the smoke and water, set the intention that it is cleaned from all who might have touched it. Know that it is reset to work for you and your purposes. After the cleansing, sit on the ground, this can be inside or out, location isn't important. Relax, close your eyes and envision your intention. What is it you are protecting? Are you making a shield from other people's energy? Whatever it is, hold the idea in your mind. Clap your hands together and start rubbing them back and forth. As your palms heat up, feel your intention build in your hands. When you're ready, start pulling your hands apart. Envision a ball of your energy forming between them. See the color of your ball. Roll it around in your palms. Then set the energy onto the talisman. Feel as your energy and the talisman become one. Envision your intention flowing with the energy into the item. This is the simplest way to create a talisman and charge something with your vibration and intentions.

> **Note:** When taking part in suggested magick found in this book, don't hesitate to make it your own. If you like an idea but want to personalize it, that is exactly what you should do.

Hexwards

There are other ways to create wards that have a little bit more kick to them. Much like a firearm someone might keep in their home, not all wards have to be in action all the time. You wouldn't pull out a pistol and show it to your friends, not if you're responsible. But you have that gun just in case you need to protect yourself or your family in a crisis. There are wards you can set for the same purpose. These are safeguards that deliver a little instant reciprocity at the same time, a magick warning shot in the best case and returned fire in the most extreme situations.

A good defense is a great offense. That adage is a tried and true strategic principle of war. And rest assured, you are fighting a war. There are forces that every one of us must come up against every day. From chronic illness to the workplace gossip, or from bill collectors to abusers, and everything in between; all of us are in the fight of our lives. Setting up boundaries and passively guarding ourselves is just one way to ensure safety.

Another way to use a ward would be to put something in place as a protective attack. Think of it like a booby trap. The defense is set, left in the ready. If you're attacked in any way, the defenses are activated. If no one attacks, the trap is not sprung, it remains there dormant. This is a proactive way to not only protect yourself but to also ensure that another's retaliation is hindered if not completely nullified.

I call these types of wards *hexwards*. A ward is like a wall but a hexward is like a wall hiding poisonous darts. In this case, the darts are only triggered if someone walks past the wall without permission. This magick is not exactly a hex but isn't exactly a ward either. While it is undeniably protection magick, there isn't really a hex involved unless it is activated. In other words, it isn't meant to hurt anyone unless they first have the intention to hurt you. In the case that your defensive magick is triggered, the hexing is then justified.

Maybe you have a Witch friend. Perhaps they are great all the time until you disagree with them. Then strange things start to happen. You can't find your lucky bracelet, or there are issues at home. Things aren't going right in general and it's easy to feel as if you're under attack. The strained relationship is becoming harder to manage as you stand up for what you believe in, refusing to cower to another Witch's inflated sense of self. Keeping things cordial is the name of the game, especially in our small Witching community, but never at the expense of your own voice.

While you aren't completely sure, it's hard to drop the suspicion that this supposed friend is performing works against you. Action may be necessary. Not wanting to create an issue where there may not be one, a hexward seems like the best idea, for now. If you get a call from this person about how some horrible thing happened to them, you'll know what's really going on.

If this Witch is doing any magick against you, protection would be in place. However, in the off-chance that there is nothing to worry about, a larger mess is not created by working magick against them unnecessarily. If a ward is necessary it would certainly be more efficient to also include a counterattack, just to ensure that this Witch gets what they deserve for messing with you in the first place. As long as they aren't working against you, the magick isn't triggered. But should they try anything with your protective attack in place, you will definitely know that your decision to place this hexward was a solid choice.

TRY THIS
Don't Cross Me, Witch

Here is a hexward I have put in place when dealing with a situation much like the one I just described.

A word of warning: If you're going to bury anything in a graveyard, do it away from actual graves. In most states, burying or digging up soil from a graveyard is illegal. You don't want to disturb the dead, and it's pretty disrespectful on a human level to go around messing with the final resting place of any dead thing. Also just as important is to protect yourself before entering the graveyard. Carry a clean and clear crystal meant to absorb negativity. As you leave the cemetery repeat the words, "Nothing can follow me; nothing can attach." As you reach the boundary of the graveyard, cast your crystal away from you. This will send anything attached to the crystal out of your life. As you leave the crystal behind, do not look back.

Also, there are likely laws against doing this type of work. Be as discreet as possible and aim for the outer edge of the cemetery, as it is easier to go unnoticed. The older the graveyard the better. If you are not allowed to enter the cemetery because there are rules when visitors are allowed in, you're best off finding a more suitable location. Keep in mind that you are running the risk of getting caught and you might end up in trouble. Carry out this practice at your own risk.

What You'll Need

- A container to bury
- Paper and something to write with
- Cinnamon, to speed up results and give your magick a boost
- Salt, for protective properties
- Cayenne, to reverse the effects of any nefarious magick used against you
- Chili powder, to add a kick to the retaliation portion of the spell
- Wasp's nest, to create pain and fear but also to protect against any malicious spells cast on you
- Paprika, to add energy to your spell and to cause trouble should your hexward become activated
- An offering to leave behind, it should be biodegradable and not pose any danger to the location.

The Process

On the paper, write the name of the person you believe you need protection from, then write, "If you cross me it will sting and burn." Place the paper into your container. Surround the paper with equal portions of salt, cinnamon, cayenne pepper, chili powder, ground up wasp nest, and paprika. Do this until the container is full. Seal your container and write the person's name on it as well.

Bury the spell in a graveyard and leave an offering for the spirits of the cemetery on top of your burial place. Your spell is now at rest but will function like a seed. If it is activated, it will sprout and cause the person crossing you pain and suffering.

Sweeten Up

Some Witches aren't comfortable with the idea of an attack of any sort. These are the types that prefer a more loving approach. While my vibration is set at a frequency that leads to a more aggressive course of action, I would be remiss to assume that all Witches should engage in these actions. Furthermore, to believe that there is only one way to deal with anyone who is attacking me would be a grave mistake on my behalf. Often there are several available routes one could take in guarding themselves against the nefarious endeavors of others.

Sometimes we need people to be kinder to us. Other times we just need them to be agreeable. Perhaps you have a boss who is a tyrant and you think needs a little attitude adjustment. In a more extreme situation, you might need to alter a person's behavior for your own safety. Honey jars are a great way to protect yourself. While they can be used in several other ways, I have found that using one to help a person sweeten up to me is efficient.

A honey jar spell can be used for several different intentions. Typically you might find Witches using them for spells where they are trying to get a job, a raise, a lover, a new friend, or to gain favoritism. Protection is an often overlooked use for such a spell. Consider how valid it is to protect one's self by helping a person become more kind to them. A bully is much less likely to bully a person they are fond of. Beyond that, sometimes it isn't physical harm that we may need protection from. It is possible that what we need to protect is our position or circumstance.

What if you were in college? The schedule of classes next semester comes out and the professor who teaches Biology is a jerk who never grades fairly. Friends who have had them as a professor all have the same story. They get excellent grades all the time but when they took this teacher's class, they felt like the grading was more harsh than necessary. Most of them barely made it out of the class with an eighty percent.

What you're going to need to do is to make the professor like you. This is very much affecting the teacher's free will, and there are ethics involved in this sort of magick that some Witches might not agree with. Controlling a person is not always fair. With access to magick that could do this sort of thing, it is important to be responsible. Often in the world we will find that not everyone will like us. It is our duty as Witches to know when we should or should not attempt to control a person's feelings. In other words, no one should have fifty different honey jars working just to ensure that they are well liked by all the people they know. This sort of spell is one that requires a Witch to be discerning about the difference between their wants and their needs. If you absolutely need this person to like you in order to protect yourself, this is the spell to use. If you just want to be liked for the sake of popularity, it is best to work on yourself more than the free will of another person.

This procedure can be used for many things. Whether it is to cause a person to care for you, grow a friendship, get a specific job, encourage a raise at work, or fend off an abuser. It is important to apply the right tag lock. A tag lock is something that connects your spell to the person you are working it on. You can write your intention on a piece of paper when all else fails, but having an item that signifies the target of the spell gives it the extra boost that's always helpful.

Slow Like Honey, Sweeten Their Mood

This honey jar spell will help to sweeten a person's attitude towards you.

What You'll Need

- A tag lock

- A container, preferably glass but as long as it will hold the honey, anything will work

- Honey, to sweeten them up. If you don't have honey, sugar water, or syrup will work in a pinch.

The Process

Write your intention for the honey jar on the tag lock. This will help to set it into the spell. For example, "grade me fairly" or "hire me for this job I deserve." It is simple and to the point. The endeavor is not to gain something that isn't earned, just to enhance your chances of getting what you want.

Next take a jar of honey or an old jar filled with sugar water or syrup—anything sweet works. Into the jar place the tag lock and then seal it. Set the vessel in the window; both the energy of the sun and the moon will help your intention grow. It will warm the liquid in the container during the day and add the power of the moon and stars at night. To ensure no negative energy finds its way into your spell, you could set it on a plate of salt to act as a boundary. It's also important to put the jar in a place where no one else can touch it.

Each day, take the time to hold the honey jar. Roll it around in your hands and speak kindly to it. Give gratitude for the intention you have set coming to fruition, and mention all the things you like about your intended target. Be sure to only say nice things to the jar and always be thankful. Keep the energy coming into the working as pure and positive as you can. Continue this process every day and watch the results appear. Once you have received what you want, bury the jar to put the spell to rest.

Put It on Ice

Just as the honey jar works well for protecting things in your life from people, there are other spells to help you keep things in your life. Conversely, it may sometimes be more efficient to send people and things away, or you might find it necessary to simply stop a person in their tracks—in other words, freeze them.

I am a huge fan of the freezer spell and here's why. I love the Queen of Swords, a tarot card sometimes associated with a cold-hearted, bitchy attitude. When I have been crossed or done wrong, I embody this card with every part of my being. The noble Queen of Swords represents the idea that you can basically freeze a person out of your life, and that is exactly what a freezer spell can do for you.

I've seen this type of spell used for all sorts of stuff, from keeping things exactly the way they are to ensuring a special deal at the store remains available until you get there. As is the case with any spell, it's all about your intentions and how you work it.

Everyone has a person they need to cut ties with at some point in our lives. They may become toxic, condescending, or abusive. When it reaches the point where we have had enough, the mundane action of ghosting on them is sometimes not enough. This is when a freezer spell can be most effective. The intention behind a spell like this is to literally freeze a person out. Because this is already something we are likely trying to do in our daily lives by not answering their calls or blocking them on social media, the support for the spell is typically already in place.

Protection isn't always about getting rid of someone; sometimes we want to protect what we have. A freezer spell can also be used for this endeavor. For instance, in matters of the heart we are often vulnerable and tend to experience fear. This can happen when the person we love has an ex who pops back into their life. Even if we trust them, it wouldn't be abnormal to worry a little that the ex has a motive to interfere with our relationship.

A freezer spell could be used in this situation as well. Instead of freezing the ex out, the intention of the spell is to freeze the feelings of our relationship in place. The goal is to put the romantic feelings in a state of stasis. They won't grow, but they won't fade either. This sort of spell will only protect what you currently have. This means that if your partner has feelings for the other person that are stronger than the ones they have for you, the outcome may not be in your favor. Use caution when performing a spell like this because it is very possible that you won't get what you want out of it. It's also important to remember not to expect a lot of forward movement with this type of spell.

If you decide to use a freezer spell, keep in mind that this style of magick can carry with it profound effects. Stopping anything in its tracks isn't easy. Imagine the force it takes to stop a train or even a rolling ball. While crafting the spell may not take a lot of effort, the energy it will draw from you at first may be significant. With that said, be sure to add some self-care into your practice for at least a few days after performing the spell.

TRY THIS
Cold as Ice

This spell will help you freeze a person out of your life.

What You'll Need
- A container, anything freezer safe will work
- A tag lock of the person or thing you want to get rid of
- Your urine

The Process
Always start by creating your tag lock. This could be something the person gave you or simply their name written on a piece of paper. Place the tag lock into the container and then urinate into it. This is your symbolic gesture that the person in mind is a waste to you. Just like we excrete the things we don't need; we are removing the person. While filling the container, picture your life free of this person. Imagine the relief of never interacting with them again. Finally, seal the container while envisioning the spell at work.

Once the container is sealed, place it in the freezer. It is best to put the container in the back behind other things so that you don't see it often. The idea is that while the spell is doing its job, you aren't thinking about it.

It is important that as long as the spell is in place, you don't interact with the person in question. Even if they reach out, you must ignore them for the attempts of contact to cease. When the spell is finished, you can bury the container like you would anything that has died. Do this somewhere far away from where you live. A cemetery would be best, but anywhere not on your land is fine.

TRY THIS
Frozen in Time

This spell will help you keep something frozen in place.

What You'll Need
- A container, anything freezer safe will work
- A tag lock, something associated with the thing you want to keep in place. For love, rose quartz is a good choice along with a picture of the two of you. If it is an item you want to buy, use an image of it. The goal for the tag lock is whatever locks the spell to your intention.
- Yarrow, for protection

The Process
Fill the container with water. As you do this, place your intentions into the water to work like a fortress that will protect your desired thing in time. Hold your tag lock and whisper to it, telling it that it is yours and that you will be back for it when the time is right. Tell the tag lock to wait for you and not to change in any way. Then imagine the desired outcome frozen in place. Finally add the yarrow to the container so that it will protect whatever it is that you are freezing in place.

When you are ready to release the spell from holding what you have frozen, take the container out and let it sit in the sun. Allowing the spell to thaw naturally will set into motion a natural reemergence of forward movement. Slowly letting things move back to their normal pace is ideal after freezing them in place

If you have frozen a relationship in place, when the spell is thawed out it would be a great opportunity to take the tag lock that you froze and move it to a honey jar. Doing so will help jump-start the relationship and help it grow stronger.

A Conscious Optimist

Whether you are a perfect trust type or a conscious optimist like me, protecting yourself is always valid. Taking precautions to keep yourself safe does not mean that you are phobic in any way—it means you are being responsible. When you take all the necessary steps to ensure that you are safe spiritually, emotionally, and physically, you are participating in self-care.

Whatever type of protection you choose to use, always remember that you are doing these things for *you*. Witchcraft is all about bettering yourself and your situation. However, never forget that if you are in a bad place, need instant protection, or there is danger, seek help. There is nothing wrong with mundane behavior. Witches are powerful but even so, sometimes a situation can be larger than anything we are able to handle.

Suggested Reading

Practical Protection Magick: Guarding and Reclaiming Your Power by Ellen Dugan. Llewellyn Publications, 2010.

The Witch's Shield: Protection Magick & Psychic Self-Defense by Christopher Penczak. Llewellyn Publications, 2004.

5
Tarot Is a Tool

I love tools. As bizarre a statement as this may seem, it is my truth. My favorite place to shop is the hardware store. I see things like drills, impact drivers, circular saws, or orbital sanders and I get noticeably excited. This passion of mine goes beyond the idea of traditional tools as well. As it turns out, a tool can be just about anything. From the name of a prog-rock band whose music opens the minds of mosh-pitting masses, to the phone I am typing on now; the word *tool* has one meaning under which hundreds of thousands of things can be classified. Tools assist with an action we are attempting to accomplish.

The tarot is a tool in this way. The cards help us learn, teach, understand, and grow while veiled behind the mystery of metaphor. On the surface, the tarot is just a set of cards with fancy art on them. It is that art that makes them special, though. The images span the entirety of the human condition. In these cards we find a complete story. Birth, death, and everything that could happen in between can all be found within this magical tool. Typically Witches turn to their tarot cards for divination, although tarot's uses are dynamic; they can be used for simple activities such as in card-guided meditation or in complex spell work. The tarot can be used to fuel creativity or act as an instrument to enhance our intuition.

Sometimes reading the tarot can be intimidating. Divination is the action of gaining guidance or insight for a situation. It is a supernatural connection to the unseen world around us. Tapping into that energy is not only overwhelming for some but is also itself an uncomfortable idea for others. Beyond that, learning the meaning of seventy-eight different cards can seem like a daunting task. While these feelings are valid, they are unfounded. We all start somewhere. It isn't our beginnings that matter but rather the paths we take to get beyond that point. My introduction to tarot was in 1999.

My Story: Urban Survivalist

The world was supposed to come to a screeching halt at the end of 1999. It had something to do with all the computers not being able to handle the number 2000. This supposedly was going to end civilization as we knew it. I could not have cared less. My whole life fit inside of a book bag; the rest of the world was pretty low on my list of concerns. I wore JNCO jeans tattered at the feet and stained with sidewalk sludge coupled with a black Adidas shirt. The other two outfits in my backpack consisted of a pair of baggy cargo shorts, a white tank-top undershirt, a zebra print button-up shirt, and a regular pair of jeans. The only objects in my bag otherwise were my journal and a deck of tarot cards.

Finally considered an adult, I was free. Even though I was homeless, there was joy in the fact that there would be no more boy's homes, youth shelters, or treatment centers. In that freedom, Witchcraft became more accessible regardless of my limited knowledge and resources. At that point in my life I was one of those people who wanted to be a practicing Witch but was only kind of pulling that off. By "kind of," I mean I'd seek out the New Age/Occult section of some big box store, sit down on the floor cross legged, and read for hours. In my composition book I would occasionally scribble a few notes on whatever resonated with me. This was a great way to pass the day. When you have no home to escape the heat of the Texas summer sun, the comfortable anonymity of a big name book store provided all the comforts one could hope for while seeking a reprieve before nightfall.

Being homeless meant hustling. The need to make at least enough to buy a pack of cigarettes rated much higher on one's hierarchy of needs when food and shelter weren't readily available. And the hustle itself could take on many shapes and forms. For me, it never meant asking people for handouts. I believe in working for what I receive and I had a deck of tarot cards, the traditional Rider-Waite-Smith deck. After the sun went down, I would sit on the sidewalk in front of an empty storefront, dirty clothes and all, calling out to anybody walking past me. I'd holler, "Tarot readings, pay what you want. All donations accepted." Sometimes I'd luck out, more often than not I wouldn't.

Twilight would set in, as the neon of Deep Ellum flickered to life. Pink, green, purple, and blue filled the night like a dark rainbow beckoning young freaks in like the pied piper. That's what they called us back then, "freaks." That five block stretch of Main and Elm was our comfort zone. Deep Ellum was an area of Dallas located just past the highway overpass, near the city center. Our safe place was the sex, drugs, and rock-n-roll of the whole city, littered with cigarette butts and other detritus. This was our home, the only place we outsiders fit in.

Tattoo parlors, head shops, bars, and random vintage stores were the main attractions of our sanctuary, for everyone else who didn't really belong there. It was a perfect place for a street urchin to attempt a money grab with tarot readings. If anyone in the city was going to be interested, they would surely be found in Deep Ellum after sunset.

The thing about reading tarot from the sidewalk is that people don't really take you seriously. Maybe it was the way I looked, young and covered in street dirt. Perhaps it had more to do with the fact that I had no clue what I was doing. I followed the little book that comes with the cards. While it's okay to refer to the book, all of my readings rang false.

I lacked the respect which is imperative for working with the cards, as well as the intuition and knowledge necessary in order to decipher the meaning behind any spread I was pulling. Reading the tarot required practice. This was something I barely had time for. Maintaining any sort of order to my day was near impossible when I had to figure out how I would eat or where I would sleep. Not having access to fulfill my basic human needs affected everything. Given my circumstances, there was no way I could develop as a Witch, let alone a tarot reader.

If I Had Known

At the time, reading tarot made a lot of sense. Sitting on the sidewalk yelling at passers-by was an immature approach but it seemed novel to me. I'm not the first person to attempt to make money this way, but it was a failed endeavor for several reasons. For starters, tarot demands respect. The energy we put into the cards is what connects us to the Source, which is what helps us understand the reading. As an eighteen-year-old street kid, I barely respected myself let alone the cards. Attempting to read for people was a decision I had made on a whim. If I had known then that with a little effort and some time I could have given readings that resonated with people, I would have taken the tarot more seriously from the start.

Tarot itself started as a game when the decks were first created. What I was doing wrong at the time was treating it like it was still a game. It was a novelty, in hindsight. I wanted to be serious about everything Witchy but couldn't be expected to pull that level of seriousness off. On the streets you don't have a place to build an altar, nor is there a safe place to sit and meditate to fill your cards with your energy. In poverty, it is near impossible to find the time to really learn all the ins and outs of something like the tarot. How could you? When you're busy surviving, that's your main goal.

What I have learned since those street days is that the tarot is a tool I could use to better myself first. Giving readings to others is a sidecar to the true purpose of tarot and magick, which is self improvement. With maturity and a stable lifestyle, I have learned that what I have to gain from the tarot has much more to do with divining my path and its purpose. When I pull cards for myself now, I am attempting to understand my higher self, hear my inner voice, listen to the Source and the messages it is trying to deliver to me.

Reading tarot for others comes eventually for some people but never manifests for others. I am not a tarot reader in the sense that I actively give out readings. I have a strong daily practice of pulling cards, turning to them in moments of confusion or uncertainty. There are plenty of people who choose to make tarot reading a career, usually because they are called to do so. For me, the tarot is a personal device that allows me to look deeper into myself and my own situations.

I enjoy practicing with my friends and my sister. I often have a message for those whom I chose to pull for, but I am not a tarot reader. What I am is a Witch who happens to use one of the many tools at my disposal to perform magick. The tarot does a lot more for me than tell me what to expect out of my day. The cards make me aware of things I am hiding from myself. They help me see the true nature of things that I am feeling. And they help me understand the world around me.

I have come a long way from the boy in dirty clothes on the street corner. I have developed my understanding of the tarot to a point that I use them in a number of ways now. I cast spells with my older decks and set altars with intentions focused around the meaning of a card. I have learned to understand the meaning of a card as it relates to a situation or a subject as opposed to depending on what the little book tells me. More than anything, I have learned that the tarot is more than a bunch of cards for parlor tricks. I have learned that the tarot is a meaningful and valid ally in the battle we all face against the world.

Learning the Basics

Tarot cards are traditionally made up of two types of cards, the major arcana and the minor arcana. Each has a message to deliver, and that message could appear in a number of ways. Sometimes a single card can tell us what we need to know, while other times it takes a complete spread to really receive the message. The entire deck is diverse, not only in the information each card presents but also in the story they tell when pulled in groups. The major and minor arcana work in concert with each other based on their positions in a spread and in the directions in which they are laid out. Learning the basics will help any budding practitioner.

Major Arcana

The major arcana is made up of twenty-two cards. These cards are meant to speak on our relationship to the universe. In other words, the major arcana tells us how we are relating to the bigger picture, how our souls are affected by the universal laws. These are the big lessons we are or should be learning in this life. They tend to shed light on the deeper things we tend to ignore.

Minor Arcana

The minor arcana are much more about our human experience; how we as humans are relating to the world around us. There are fifty-six of these cards. They are separated into four suits. With fourteen cards per suit, the suits can vary from deck to deck but there are almost always several correspondences they are associated with. The typical suits are: wands, swords, pentacles/disks/coins, and finally cups.

Suit Correspondences

	Cups	Wands	Pentacles	Swords
Element	Water	Fire	Earth	Air
Zodiac	Cancer, Scorpio, Pisces	Aries, Leo, Sagittarius	Taurus, Virgo, Capricorn	Gemini, Libra, Aquarius
Direction	West	South	East	North
Symbolism	Emotions	Actions	Physical	Thoughts

While there are no bad cards, often people can feel a little trepidation when certain cards show up. An example would be the Tower card. This card speaks of a change that is coming, often one that includes a dramatic or even traumatizing event. At first it can seem like this is an omen but when you look deeper into the idea that the card presents, the sense of foreboding eases up. In the image on the card we see people falling from a structure that is typically being struck by lightning. The tower is on fire and destruction is the main focus. Looking deeper, though, we are required to take into consideration every time we have fallen. It wasn't the end of the world; we stood up, we kept going.

Other cards may seem like they present good news but they carry with them a caveat. The Wheel of Fortune, for instance, in its upright position tells us that we have reached a moment of greatness. This card speaks to the idea that, at that moment, we have all that we have asked for. But this card also serves as a reminder. Our fortune can change in the blink of an eye. We are informed by this card that everything in life moves in cycles. For now we may be at the top of the world but as sure as the sun rises every day, trouble will find its way back to us. The message is the opposite when the Wheel of Fortune is in reverse because it is all about the cycle of life; it reminds us that the hard times pass as well.

The final note to carry forward in regard to the tarot is that many of the cards have a plethora of meanings. Each card in any position can indicate several things. Their illustrations often indicate what they are trying to tell us. Beyond that, the positions, or way that the cards are laid down, have a lot to say too. Many tarot readers choose to read reversed positions. This is when the card is laid out upside down. The meanings of the cards in this position are sometimes subtle. Other times they are the complete opposite. The Judgement card always relates to a shift in our spiritual lives. When it is upright it tells us we are there now, deep in the experience. On the other hand, when it is reversed it tells us that we are close to the shift that is coming and it asks us to look into ourselves to find the thing that is holding us back.

Learning these basics took me much longer than I would have wanted it to. Honestly though, in 1999 I couldn't have been expected to take the time to learn even that much. Having known more about the tarot would have informed my random street readings. This would have helped me to be a more well rounded reader. In truth, it just wasn't my time. I heard the call of the tarot but it was only an early indicator. This was informing me that eventually the tarot would be a useful asset. It wouldn't be until much later in my life that I would have the time and stability to learn to interpret the cards intuitively. Learning to use the cards daily is what has helped my practice grow.

JOURNAL PROMPT
Write Out the Basics

Take the time to learn about all the meanings of the different suits of the cards. Make lists in your journal. Begin to identify the personality of each suit. This way when you are beginning to learn your decks you have something personal to refer to. List the things you learn about the major arcana too.

As you learn the cards, you will be sure to encounter a few that leave you unsettled every time you pull them. Begin to list the reason why this card makes you feel uneasy. Additionally, look into anything positive you can learn about these cards and keep a running list of that as well. This way when you come upon those cards you can refer to your list and remember that each card has multiple meanings for you to decipher.

Your Cards Are Your Cards

The biggest mistake I made when I was on the streets was that I had no respect for the cards. I viewed them like a game, a toy I'd casually pull out for entertainment's value. This is a mistake a lot of new tarot readers make. Getting a new deck is like meeting a human in a lot of ways. No two decks are exactly the same. They can have the same packaging and they might have been printed in the same place at the same time but they tend to come with a personality of their own.

Just because I am using the same deck as a friend sitting next to me doesn't mean that my cards will present the same sort of answers as my friend's deck might. What I mean is, my connection is different with my deck than a friend's connection might be with theirs. Sometimes you can meet people who use the same deck and they will agree that the cards are a straightforward or no-nonsense sort of deck. But other times you can talk to that same person about a different deck and you both have completely different experiences with the cards.

In this way, tarot cards can have personalities. This is the main reason you want to spend time getting to know your deck. You might learn that one of your decks does not like to let you read for other people, while another may only work when you are reading for others.

When it comes to choosing a deck, it is important to make sure you are getting the right one for you. Many Witches have more than one deck and often each one has its own reason why that Witch obtained it. Using your clairsense can help when

finding your first deck and even all the subsequent decks there-
after. The energy of the cards is typically present from the beginning. When finding a deck that is right for you be sure to hold
the deck in your hands. Look at the imagery in the deck and try
to see if it works for you. Your tarot are as much a part of your
personality as you are a part of theirs. If you don't feel a connection to the deck it might not be the right one for you.

Some Witches won't let people touch their cards while others
prefer to get the querents' energy on their cards each time. I like
to keep selenite and rose selenite on my personal deck. I also
won't read for anyone else with these cards. In addition to my
personal cards I keep a set that is meant for other people, and
I don't spend as much time putting my energy in them. This is
because when I read other people I like to let them shuffle the
cards. There isn't a wrong way to do any of this. It is all about
what resonates for you with your cards.

A daily practice of reading your tarot is the only way you are
going to learn these sorts of things. I know a lot of people, both
Witches and non-Witches, who have different ways of making
their decks their own. Some will do a smoke cleansing each time
they read with them. Others may just knock on the deck to clear
it. When it comes down to it, you create your own practice. You
will only get there, though, by developing that practice over time
and with a lot of patience.

TRY THIS
Buy Your First Deck

The internet is full of imagery of the tarot available in the world
today. There really is a deck for everyone. For this exercise, seek
out and research which one is right for you. Beyond Waite-Smith

or Thoth-inspired decks are oracle cards and Lenormand decks, to name a few.

If cartomancy, the act of divination through reading the cards, is calling to you, know which cards you seek to read.

Occult and metaphysical shops everywhere often carry a variety of decks to choose from. Sit with the decks. Look over the imagery, feel what calls to you. Allow your clairsenses to inform you as to what deck you should obtain. Do you get a sense when you pick up the deck? Is there a gut reaction, a smell, or even a sound as you hold the deck in your hands? Do you pick up a deck and know this is the one? These are the beginnings of your deck's relationship with you. When you find the best fit, buy them for yourself.

TRY THIS
With a New Deck

Let your cards sit on an altar for a while. Whether you have a working altar or one that is dedicated to a deity, this is your place of power, a single location where your vibration and that of the Source's come together to become one. Give your deck time to soak in that energy so that the cards become one with you and the Source as well. The amount of time you leave your cards in this place of power will differ for everyone. Some like to do this on the full or new moon. Others might let their cards sit in their power place for a complete moon cycle. Only you know how long your cards need to soak up the energy needed to help you work with them.

If you don't keep an altar, or if you aren't able to have one, carry the cards with you. Keep them in your purse or book bag. Alternatively, if you don't have the means to carry your cards you can keep them under your pillow while you sleep and in a special place while you are out and about living your day. This special place could be in your car or even your sock drawer if that's where you keep things you don't want others to mess with. Wherever you keep things safe, however, you can infuse your own vibration into this tool; it's the best way for you to make the cards yours.

TRY THIS
Before Using the Deck

On a full moon, go out into the night. Under the light of the moon, sit with your new deck in your hands. Breathe deeply and clear your mind as much as you can. Be in that moment; whatever has happened and whatever may need your attention later doesn't matter. You can ground yourself if you choose.

Focus on the light of the moon, feel it fill your body with its magickal energy. Picture its light running through your veins, your bones, notice the way your vibration begins to sync up with the moon's vibration. As you feel the energy of the moon coursing through your body use your mind to collect it all into one place. This can be your head, or your heart, whatever resonates with you. Then take that energy and push it down into your hands where you've been holding the cards. As the energy resides in your hands, force it into the cards. You have drawn down the magick of the moon and placed them in the cards, effectively charging them. You could recharge them once a month or as needed from this point forward.

A Strong Daily Practice

Maybe you play a musical instrument, or you're an artist. Perhaps you participate in sports, or skateboard for fun. You might be a lawyer, a doctor, a chef, HR manager, or any number of professions. No matter what you do, whether it's your spare-time activity or a full-time job, it takes daily practice to get good at what you're doing. Tarot works in exactly the same way. It is imperative to put effort into learning the cards if you want to become good at deciphering their messages.

A strong daily practice is essential if you really want to read the Tarot. Getting familiar with the cards is important in order to truly understand them. I'm not saying you have to memorize all of the meanings to each card. Eventually you'll get there but this is something that will take you years to master. What you want to do is treat your deck like you would a new friend. Respecting the cards in this way helps to create a sense of reciprocity between the two of you.

A practitioner would learn best by making time for their cards. This means that no matter what, you sit down with your tarot each and every day. For me, this is typically after I have woken up and had a few cups of coffee. Sometimes I don't get to my deck until much later in the day. That's okay, as long as I do in fact get to my cards at some point during the day. Practicing with your cards creates a bond between the two of you that allows for messages to flow more freely.

Practice can take on several different looks. From shuffling and pulling two cards, to laying out a full spread. How you practice can only be decided by you. What happens when you are practicing in this way is a couple different things, the most important of which is learning the cards themselves, their personality and the type of messages they deliver.

A Card a Day

The best beginner practice I know of is to pull one card a day. When you shuffle your cards and pull one, you get a simple message that will either ring true or it won't. This is a great way to start becoming familiar with the cards while creating a habit that will enhance your practice.

A Picture Says So Much

When you pull your daily card, don't start by reading about it. Look at the picture. How do you feel when you see this image? Does it stir any sort of emotion in you? When building a daily practice, it is important to learn how the cards make you feel. Identifying your feelings with the cards will connect you to your daily practice on an emotional level and help to inspire you to be consistent with your practice every day.

Buddy Readings

Creating a formidable daily practice isn't easy. Finding a friend with similar interests will not only give you someone to share your experience with but it will also provide you with someone to hold you accountable. Practicing anything daily can become tedious and cumbersome. When you have a friend to share readings with, you will not only gain insight from someone else while you are learning but it will be less of a chore and more of a social event.

Don't Start with Questions

It would be great to have all our burning questions answered clearly. Don't start there though. When you ask your tarot a question, it can be disheartening to get an answer you don't want or, worse, one you don't understand. Instead of asking your cards for a direct answer each day, go to the cards with an open mind. I get the best results on my daily readings when I simply question what it is I need to know right now. Even if the answer is ambiguous, I am not placing the weight of the world on a clear answer. Typically when I maintain an open mind with the cards, the meaning becomes clear as my day moves forward.

Becoming Familiar with the Cards

When you pull cards daily, you start becoming familiar with the cards. The more your practice grows, the more cards you come across. Eventually you will pull every card at least once. For beginners, this is commonly a vital way to learn. Someone just starting out will likely be reading meanings from a book or online. As they repeatedly read the same meanings, those descriptions become committed to memory.

Learning to understand the cards goes beyond shuffling and pulling them, it goes further than reading their meanings. When I pull cards in the morning, I have the whole day to think about their meaning. The reading doesn't end when the cards are put away because we carry their message with us regardless of what we do next. When I get to work and learn that a coworker has gone behind my back to pitch an idea I told them about in passing, I begin to understand why I pulled the Seven of Swords, a card that typically represents betrayal and deception.

Reading the tarot requires effort and dedication. It demands that the reader take time to understand how one card correlates to another. The Tower is about destruction and the Empress is about new life. If the two are paired together, a clear story is being told. When read separately, the nuance in their relationship in the spread is lost. In this way, understanding your cards is vital for a more accurate depiction of what they are trying to say.

TRY THIS
Learning the Card Meanings

In this exercise I offer two options: one for beginners, and one a challenge for those readers experienced with the tarot.

For Beginners

For seventy-eight days, pull one card off of the top of the deck—do not shuffle the cards to ensure that over the next seventy-eight days, you will interact with every card in the deck. Read the description of the card. You can turn to the internet if you like and get a more in-depth overview of the card's meaning. Then carry that meaning with you throughout the day. Ponder it. What would the literal meaning of the card be? And if it were a metaphor, how could it pertain to your day? Nothing is off of the table; consider the card in every interaction you have. You may find that the card of the day means nothing at first, or you might see that when juxtaposed against every interaction, a meaning eventually develops. At the end of the day, read the description again one last time. Think about its message and see if you can identify the ways it applied to your life for that one day. Then place the card at the bottom of the deck and move onto a new card the next day.

For Experienced Readers

For seventy-eight days, pull the top card off of your deck and read the description. Maybe you haven't needed to do this for some time, but reacquaint yourself with the card's meaning. Then take time during the day to consider the card. How many times in your life have you had a scenario that this card speaks about? How many times have you pulled this card only to see its meaning come into fruition? When you pull this card in a reading, do you have a gut reaction? Is this card one you like to see, or does it cause anxiety? Are your feelings about this card sound, or are they biased? For that day, dive deep into the meaning of the card and your personal relationship to it. Is this a relationship dynamic enough to openly fluctuate each time you pull the card, or are you actively resisting the meaning based on past pulls? Is that fair? Could you change your perspective? After you pull the card, place it at the bottom of the deck and move on to a new card the next day.

Reading the Cards Intuitively

Intuition can play a large role in tarot reading. Intuitive reading is when you look at the cards and decipher the meaning from the images you see there. In this case, you are able to learn the card quickly without worrying about the traditional meaning of the card. With every deck, illustrations on the cards vary. I only deal with the Waite-Smith and similar decks, but even then the imagery can differ from the traditional deck depending on the artist. In this case, you may read a description for the card typical to any deck but when reading only the image on the card, it might tell a completely different story. This would be the perfect situation for reading the cards intuitively.

With some cards, intuitive reading can be easy. The Hanged Man, for instance, is a man hanging upside down with a fairly relaxed expression. According to most definitions in books on tarot card meanings, this card is often related to finding new perspective or if reversed, possibly indecision. But when you look closer at the card, you see a man who is relaxed in either position. His hands are typically behind his head as if he is resting, giving a feeling of taking a break. When I come across the Hanged Man in a reading, my first thought is always to pause.

Sometimes the meaning of a card is not so clear in the illustration. The Moon is described as a card of illusion. The most common interpretation is about something hidden or the idea that things are not what they seem. When we look at the image on this card, however, it almost never seems to present that feeling. Typically there are two wolves howling at the moon in the sky. In the background are two towers, and the moon itself is shown as full with a crescent inside of it. There is almost always water in this card as well as what looks like a lobster crawling from the stream. If we were reading this card based only on the image, would your first thought be deception? Mine's not.

If I were to throw the book out the window, I would receive a completely different message from this card based on the illustration alone. Does that mean that my intuitive reading of this card is wrong? Absolutely not. What it means is that this card has a different meaning for me than it might for any other person looking at it. If I were the person reading this card for someone else and my interpretation resonated with them, then that was the message they were meant to hear.

The point behind an intuitive reading is not to get lost in the meaning some other person has attached to the card but instead to allow your own meaning to develop. When you do this you are able to find a new understanding of a card that perhaps only you can see. This is magick at work because now the message delivered is unique for both the reader and the person receiving the reading.

When you read the card intuitively, you are tapping into your clairsenses. You might have a sense of knowing or a lingering scent in your nostrils when looking over the cards you've pulled. These are indicators of what the card might be trying to tell you. Intuition is after all connected to our clairsenses. It stands to reason that a portion of those magickal senses are being put to use when we let go of what others have attributed to the cards.

The art on the cards tells us what is happening but the thing about art is that it is subjective. What I find beautiful and meaningful others may not. But that is exactly why an intuitive read is so magickal. What I see in the cards is likely different from what my sister would see, even if we are looking at the same cards. This doesn't mean either of us are wrong. It means we are each receiving an individual message from the same card.

When reading the card intuitively for yourself or someone else, it is important to take into consideration the other contributing factors surrounding the reading. What other cards are present? Do they combine to tell a story? What was the question that inspired the reading? Can it be answered through the pictures on the cards? Finally, what stands out to you, the reader, at that moment?

One of the decks I own is very colorful and surreal. Sometimes I can be looking at a card that I have seen a thousand times only to notice something in it that I have never seen before. This is when what I am seeing, what I take notice of the most, holds the message. That thing that stands out to me is significant for the reading. When something specific stands out at any point in a reading, it must pertain to what the reading is about, otherwise why would it stand out?

TRY THIS
Using Intuition

Pull a card from the deck. Focus only on the picture you see. What is it telling you? What details stand out for you? Do any of the images on the card resonate with you? Write down all of your feelings and impressions about the card. If you are familiar with the tarot try to forget everything you know and listen to only your intuition. Decipher the meaning based solely on the image. After you have written down everything you notice and feel about the card, then look up its meaning. How similar is your interpretation compared to the description you've looked up? Which meaning resonates with you more?

Not Trying to See the Future

Divination is often described as the practice of seeking knowledge of the future or the unknown by supernatural means. I am not trying to see the future when using divination. When I turn to the cards, what I am trying to do is understand my present. My belief in free will causes me to doubt the validity of any sort of prophesying.

When pulling cards, aim for understanding. Try asking what the energy around getting a new job looks like as opposed to asking if you will get a specific job. Because of free will, our lives are in a constant state of flux. This means that the cards may say that you're going to get a job you really want but sometimes, right after the cards are pulled, the circumstances will have changed in some way. At the moment you drew the spread, you might have been the best candidate but perhaps a better applicant applied before you ever got a call back. The cards can't dictate the free will of others any more than anything else. Our decisions and the decisions of others affect the paths we walk. At any moment, our journey can easily change from the outcome the cards foretold. For this reason, stay away from predictive card pulls, opting instead for ones centered around clarity.

In my experience, divination is much more about guidance than it is about seeing the future. Using any form of divination to receive guidance has always worked out best for me. Oftentimes I have attempted divination for specific future events and inevitably found myself let down and questioning my own Witchcraft.

Questions for the Cards

When seeking guidance it is important to know what kind of questions to ask your tarot. Instead of asking things like, "Will this person fall in love with me?" you could rephrase the question and say, "What can I do in order to find the love I am seeking?" Instead of asking for some insight on the future, you are asking for information to help you grow and become more in touch with your true inner self.

The questions we ask are important, they can make or break the reading. When I was a street kid, I would ask people what they wanted to know. I fully believed, at the time, that I was helping others look into the future. I had no idea how to formulate a question in order to help others or myself find the answers they sought. Now I understand the difference between a productive question and a poorly phrased one.

Productive questions are ones where you leave the door open for whatever might come through. For instance, How can I best navigate the health system in order to find relief from my disease? would be productive, whereas What can I do about my disease? is poorly phrased. While both questions have merit, the first is well thought out and indicates that you already have a plan but need some additional guidance. The latter question is more like reaching blindly into a bag while hoping you pull out a helpful solution.

Some readers do well with direct yes or no questions. Because the querent is seeking a predictive response, I prefer to avoid questions like this. Other readers function best with more ambiguous questions. This way, the answer functions not as a prediction but more like a map of how to reach a goal. A friend once told me to instead try asking what the energy around a situation is. This has proven to be an extraordinarily useful approach.

There are mornings when I sit on my bed, still slightly groggy. I don't have a question but I want to maintain my daily practice. In these moments I just ask, What do I need to know right now? Other times when I think I have no questions or I am trying to focus on something specific. I will inevitably let my mind wander onto something else. I find in these moments I tend to end up with cards that are responding to my wandering thoughts. This is like a pure message from the Source. These types of reading are the best for me because they are truthful and organic answers to something that may have been bothering me.

Develop Tarot Reading Skills

I began my tarot practice during a rough time in my life. It wasn't the most ideal moment to dive into anything let alone something like tarot. More than two decades later, I am able to devote the time it takes to develop tarot reading skills. These skills did not come overnight. There are times even now when anyone may have to stop and refer to a card's meaning. There are bound to be days when you really don't care to participate in your own practice—but do it anyway.

Take time each day, even if it is for only one card. Look at it and attempt to discern its meaning. Think about ways to make your practice stronger by developing themes for a week on what sort of guidance you are after. And write everything down. Every question you ask and every card you pull can be written in a book dedicated to your practice, and your practice will be stronger for it. If I look back a year or two or four in my tarot journal, I can see how much I have grown. Journaling your tarot experience is one sure-fire way to not only hold yourself accountable but also to see how far you've come. Whether you have been reading the cards for years or you are only just beginning, keeping a book with all your readings in them is just another way to develop your practice into a formidable one. Over time, seeing where you started in comparison to where you've come will be all it takes to keep you moving forward.

Suggested Reading

Intuitive Tarot: 31 Days to Learn to Read Tarot Cards and Develop Your Intuition by Brigit Esselmont. IngramSpark, 2019.

Holistic Tarot: An Integrative Approach to Using Tarot for Personal Growth by Benebell Wen. North Atlantic Books, 2015.

Kitchen Table Tarot: Pull Up a Chair, Shuffle the Cards, and Let's Talk Tarot by Melissa Cynova. Llewellyn Publications, 2017.

6
Mundane Work Is Spell Work Too

There is magick in persistence and in working for what you want to achieve. One basic aspect of spell crafting is all the effort you put into it. Research, candle making, collecting herbs, setting altars, and making tools for rituals is a big part of creating magick that works. But there is a much larger aspect that even I have been guilty of falling short on, and that is doing the work.

The word "work" brings to mind hard labor or begrudgingly doing duties that are necessary but unappealing. Resentment is often a companion to the idea of toiling through a day on the job. Most people (Witches included) lack the luxury of freedom from working to make a living. Those of us who aren't fortunate enough to love our jobs aren't enthused when we hear the word "work." Nevertheless, we endure because we have mouths to feed, debts to pay off, and rent to make. But what would our lives be like if we redirected a fraction of the effort exerted in our work to something we deemed valuable to us?

If you didn't have to pay bills or go to work, what would you put your efforts into? Many people want a nice house or their favorite car, clothes that show off their personality, or a comfortable life for their family. They might work hard to achieve these things. What would happen to their magick if they put some of their energy there instead?

The magick of persistence is a real thing. It is the most visible aspect of the effort to manifest a desire. The value of what is wanted is weighted by how much energy is put into seeing it come to pass. When I say doing the work is the most important part of magick, I am not using a metaphor. Acquiring what we want, no matter what it is, won't come easy. Otherwise it isn't worth it.

My Story: I Did What I Had to Do

When I first became homeless, most nights it was easy to find a friend's couch to crash on. At eighteen, life was a party. There were plenty of drugs, rock music, and a lot of sex to be consumed. It was easy to forget my lot in life while I was distracted by these three things. The first night I couldn't find a place to sleep brought the whole experience crashing into reality.

Three other street kids and myself figured we would find a hotel for the night. One of my companions that evening had some money and she had offered to pay for the room. We wandered around tripping on LSD for most of the night. It was all fun and games until the girl with the money decided that she would rather just have a room with her boyfriend. That meant the other guy from our group and I were left out, alone. He and I continued to keep each other company in the dark of the night, because there is strength in numbers.

Dallas was full of older men eager to take advantage of a young boy seemingly innocent to the world. Walking through

Oak Lawn, the predominantly gay area of Dallas, could be intimidating to a young gay man. The older crowd will eat up a fresh piece of meat at the first chance they get. There was a power in knowing this. Given my childhood of sexual abuse, it should come as no surprise that I've always been sexually active. I've never been shocked by the things a grown man will do to get a little action from a young hot thing. When my evening companion suggested that I could use prostitution as a means to survive, it didn't seem like that bad of an idea.

We were walking down the street and I had caught the eye of another guy walking past us. At the time, I hadn't noticed; my mind was somewhere else. But my friend saw it happen. "That guy just checked you out," he said to me. "You should see if he is looking…you could probably charge him." My friend shrugged when he said this. I thought, "Why not?" I called out to the stranger and he stopped in his tracks. I got flirty and confident in that moment. We made an agreement for fifty dollars for a half hour of my time. I was so naive at that point; I had no idea I could have asked for so much more. I followed him to his house, scared but willing to do anything in order to afford a hotel as soon as possible.

I left the stranger's house with a pager he gave me so I could pawn it. I had a hundred dollars instead of fifty and a week-long pass for the Dallas Area Rapid Transit. Walking into the sunlight of the day, I felt reborn. There was a new understanding of the power I had in sex work. Suddenly the only skill I needed in order to survive was personality and the flesh between my legs. At that moment, I didn't need a lot of skill to make money. I just needed to be handsome, keep my wits about me, and manipulate the hearts and minds of grown men with dark desires.

As a street kid, you meet a lot of people. When every night is a party, it isn't strange to end up at their houses. There were plenty of Witches coming in and out of my life at the time. One in particular decided she wanted to help me.

It was a full moon, we were in her apartment complex, outside in a garden near the pool. She called on the goddess of the moon, asking for her assistance. We petitioned for me to find a way off the streets and into a home. The goal was to get a stable roof over my head. We drank wine while we picked flowers from the garden then left them on the walk where three paths met between her apartment and the pool. We poured our wine into a cup and left it with the flowers and then stripped off our clothes and danced in the man-made waterfall that fed into the pool. The Witch told me to envision the weight of living on the streets being washed away. She told me to feel the water clean me and energize me for the next crossroad in my journey.

For us street kids, there was only one place that really mattered: the coffee bar. This was the only place we could truly fit in. Full of goths, Witches, and street kids, we could find refuge in a bottomless cup of coffee.

The owner knew who his real clientele were. He knew that our clique of misfits was what really brought in the visitors. Everyone wants to visit an exotic place. Even vanilla wants to be Rocky Road sometimes. He knew he wanted us there. We filled the place up with oddities that would attract the gawkers from out of town, or uptown, or wherever. Seventy-five cents, that bought us a bottomless cup of coffee and just like that we weren't loitering. We were patrons, like peacocks drawing people in at the zoo. We could come and go as we liked. Just don't throw away your cup.

I started going every morning when the coffee bar opened and asking the owner if there was work I could do in order to earn a little cash. I'd sweep the back patio, empty the trash, and clean the restrooms. This earned me free coffee and enough money to buy something to eat and a pack of cigarettes. Being resilient and persistent worked in my favor. It wasn't long before the owner gave me a job.

If I Had Known

The magick my midnight full moon Witch friend did for me worked. I found a job, and if I had stuck it out with that job, I could have gotten my life on track. Instead, I was more concerned with partying and getting involved in other people's drama. In the end, I failed myself and my friend because I did not do the mundane things that were imperative to help make the magick work. My goal at the crossroads on that full moon was to get off the streets. And eventually I accomplished that for a moment, because at first I tried. I went into the coffee shop every day and asked to work, I was given a job, and eventually I found people to take me in.

If I had known that persistence would get me everything I needed in life, I wouldn't have continued to flounder. I spent years after Dallas perpetuating my own demise. I was unaware that if I had just stuck to it, I could have gotten myself out of homelessness a lot faster. What I did instead was follow paths that seemed easier. I expected the Witch's magick to do the work for me and gave the minimum amount of effort needed. At the time, it felt like I was trying really hard to free myself of the shackles of street life but when I look back at it now, I know better.

Initially I started making better friends. Being behind the counter at the coffee bar helped the paying customers get to know me. These customers were not other street kids; these were couples who had real jobs and homes they lived in. They started offering me a place to shower and a place to sleep for the night. Because I was homeless and working, people wanted to help me more. I didn't have to ask for help; it was just offered because I was doing everything I could to better myself.

What I couldn't see at the time was that getting an honest job was the first step to getting my life together. It was an opportunity to start saving money. I did the right thing by going into the coffee house every day and asking to work. But after I got the job, I stopped trying. It was as if not having to prostitute any more was enough. And once I stopped trying, things went downhill. The magick stopped working. At least at first, it worked well.

Spells Take Work

We've all been met with a dilemma that feels as though some magick is needed to help resolve it. Most Witches have a process for creating spells. Whatever your process is, be it herbs, candles, petitions, sigils, or anything else, spells take work. The first thing most of us would find ourselves doing is researching items with which to craft our spell. Do certain colored candles work best for our intention? Is there an herb that corresponds to the work we are doing? These are all questions we have to answer before we even begin the spell.

After taking the time to get the research together, preparing ourselves for the spell work is essential. A lot of Witches have different ways of doing this. Some take ritual baths, others meditate, and still there are more who cleanse their space or set up an altar for their purposes. While casting the spell itself is of course a vital part of the work, it takes up the least amount of time if you take preparation and continuing efforts into consideration. The magick exists in all aspects of the crafting, from start to finish and even afterward. The spell takes plenty of work if you are opening a circle, creating a candle, or making a sigil. Putting energy into the working will obviously take something out of us. But what comes next, after the spell is cast? Do you just go about your day? I hope not, and here is why.

It would be amazing if everything we needed could be obtained through magick, unfortunately magick doesn't work this way. No one out there casts a spell and then passively waits for the manifestation of their intentions. The Witches who are seeing results are all out there beating the pavement and making things happen for themselves. They are doing the mundane work necessary to see their goals come to light.

JOURNAL PROMPT
Know Your Goal

In your journal, write out exactly what it is you want to achieve. It could be a new car, job, romantic partner, or anything else. Once you've set your sights on the endeavor, list all the things you need to do in order to make that happen. Do you have to save money, search the want ads, join a dating app? Any mundane action that could help you achieve your goal should be on this list. Knowing all the steps you would need to take if you had no magick at all is the first step to creating your spells.

Actions Create Results

You can't just send an intention out and then do nothing. Regardless of how strong your intention is, there is more to be done once you finish the spell itself. Continuing by doing the work to help manifest the intention is the next step. The expectation at this point is for mundane efforts to be used to draw our desires to us. In other words, we have to do everything we can to help the magick work.

Let's say the goal is a perfect job. The intentions are set with specific ideas of ideal employment. All the correspondences have been gathered together. The candles are the right colors, the herbs have been selected based on their properties, and the stones are laid out to help empower the magick to do its thing. The research has been done so that the right day and time for the spell work has been chosen. When that day and time arrives, the spell is performed. We can feel great about the work we've done, but if we follow up by doing nothing else, the spell is wasted energy. The goal was a job, so the next logical step is to go out and do everything possible to make the hope of this perfect job become a reality.

Twiddling thumbs, sitting at home, waiting for the opportunity to present itself is not an option. Waiting for a miracle to happen is a fool's errand. You could wait until what you want just falls into your lap, but only waiting for the magick to do its job makes it more likely that nothing will happen at all. In essence, all that has happened was some candles were lit, words were said, herbs were collected and burned, and a special time was chosen to throw an intention into the world. What *didn't* happen was anything else to help the magick work. I'm not saying that the intentions definitely won't come to fruition in this situation, but it's highly unlikely.

There is this statement I've heard applied to different spiritual beliefs. According to Christianity, the Law of Attraction, and Witchcraft, the phrase is the same, "The (enter your spiritual source here) helps those who help themselves." The idea of helping yourself seems like a no-brainer, but as it turns out this is less practiced than it should be. Magick isn't meant to be a cure-all for everything. It's a tool that helps you get where you're going. Magick is like fuel for the car on your journey. You, the driver, are the mundane actions you must take to get there. The car doesn't move because it has fuel, it moves because *you* are pushing the gas pedal and turning the steering wheel. If you weren't there to drive it, the car would go nowhere. You have to do all the work. Without your effort, the pursuit is pointless.

TRY THIS
Set Your Intention

This practice builds upon the journal prompt from earlier.

What You'll Need
- One white candle
- Something to carve the wax with

The Process
On a new moon, take your goal from the journal exercise in this chapter and condense it down into one to three words. Sit in a space where you won't be interrupted and focus on your goal. Know that the new moon is about building energy and drawing in what you want. Use that to begin drawing in your goal.

Take the candle and carve into it the few words that state your desire. For a job this could be how much you want to make, the title of the position, or even the location of the job you want. No matter your goal, you'll want to carve three basic words that really define your intention into this candle.

Once the words are in the wax, press the candle between both your hands. Envision the intention you are after. From your heart, press your intention outward through your arms and into your hands. Release it into your candle.

Once this is complete, place the candle in a safe special place. This can be anywhere as long as you identify this place as safe and special. It should be the spot where you would keep anything magickal you are working with because that's where your magickal energy gathers.

Leave the candle there until the full moon.

Your next step is to start doing the mundane work. Do you need to build a profile on a relationship site or make yourself more available for romantic encounters? Should you spruce up your résumé? Start saving money? Whatever you listed in your journal prompt earlier, these are the things you should begin doing now.

Persistence Overcomes Resistance

The effort put into your intention after the magick is cast will indicate the time it takes to see your spell come into fruition. How we go about drawing in or manifesting our desires is an indicator for how serious we are about getting what we want. If I am asking for the best possible job out there but then never search for a job, I am clearly not that interested in working. But if I search and apply for any job I find, even if I am turned down a thousand times, eventually that ideal position is going to be mine. And the fact that I was turned down so many times indicates that none of those jobs were actually perfect for me.

Through persistence after spell work, the endeavor to gain my desire at any cost is the true magick. While of course magick was used in the form of a spell, the request would have fallen on deaf ears had it not been pushed to come into being. When I was a homeless teen, I didn't enjoy having survival sex; I did it in order to survive. I didn't stop using this survival tactic before I found a better way to handle the situation, and I did not stop searching for a way out until I found one. Going to the coffee shop every day, showing the owner that I wanted to work and wasn't interested in being lazy is what got me hired on. Magick responds to our spells in the same way the coffee shop owner responded to my endeavor to better myself.

Persistence will overcome resistance—if we try and then keep going, a solution will present itself. When we use magick to manifest those solutions, it is our responsibility to get to work on finding the way out of our problem. It is our responsibility to help the magick we create help us. Because we've used magick in order to assist us, the best possible outcome is nearly guaranteed as long as we make the right choices and keep trying despite apparent defeat.

TRY THIS
Calling Your Intention into Existence

This spell is the final step in the series of practices.

What You'll Need
- A secluded, safe place
- Your white candle from the last exercise

• Candle holder

• A match or lighter

The Process

On a full moon, take your candle out of its safe and special place. It's been about two weeks at this point, and the energy placed into your candle has grown with the moon. In a place where you know you can be alone and undistracted, take your candle holder, candle, and lighter. Sit in the light of the full moon.

Know that just as the candle is assisted by its holder, your magick is assisted by your mundane actions. And be aware that just as the candle would have no flame without your match or lighter, your magick would have no power without your intention.

Set your candle into the holder and think about your intended goal. As you light your candle, envision your intention coming to fruition. While the candle burns, speak aloud the desire you are manifesting. Let the Source hear your voice. Be sure to use the three words carved into the candle, and repeat as the candle burns. Many Witches find that making a rhyme out of their intention helps. If this works for you, then do that, it isn't necessary though.

Stay with your candle until it is finished burning. As the last lights of the fire flicker know that your intention is already manifest. In this moment be aware that your magick is complete. There is still work to be done, but the energy of your spell is out in the world doing its job. Now it's time for you to go out and do all that you can to help it find the easiest and quickest path to you.

Persistence in Liminal Space

The time between casting your magick and seeing its outcome manifest is a magickal moment. This is a liminal space. It is during this in-between phase that the most magick actually happens.

Of course having faith in your magick at this time is necessary, but faith is never as easy to have as it seems. Especially when you have a strong desire for something, holding onto the belief that your magick has worked can be very difficult. But when you persist despite contrary evidence to your endeavor, you're putting a special kind of energy into your magick.

This is when the mundane things you do to see your goals manifest matter the most. It is more likely that you will feel tested during this time. You will apply for what you think is the perfect job but not get it. You will go on dates with people you think would be the best mate only to learn that they are jerks. But this is where you keep going, where you keep pushing forward. Tap into all the resources you have, leave no stone unturned. With magick in place, we are bound to find solutions as long as we are actively pursuing them.

Taking the time to acknowledge and give thanks for the failures is important too. It will help you to see the good in a situation that didn't turn out the way you expected it to. This will help to calm you down as well as remind you that not all hope is lost. Using gratitude is a great way to work through the liminal space after your magickal casting. It is also important so that you aren't carrying around negative feelings about your spell work.

There are no shortcuts in life. In any situation, it is important to be precise in your movements. As you go forward, know what your next step will be at all times. It's okay to make mistakes too, the important thing is to learn from them. If we come out of the situation only to end up in it again a few months down the road then the lesson was not learned. The real work is all about doing whatever it takes to ensure that a change is put into motion. We can perform magick to our heart's content, but if we are constantly working spells for the same reason, there is something deeper that needs to be worked on.

What I know to be true is that the best possible outcome only happens as long as resourcefulness and diligence remain in the equation. As long as the magick necessary to help has been performed and we follow through with the real-life work to handle the problem, success is certain. We all have different situations in life. No matter what happens, as long as we work towards a resolution the best outcome becomes more likely.

JOURNAL PROMPT
What Is and Isn't Working

In your journal look over your intention. Since the day you worked your magick, what has been working? List all the moments that you have glimpsed success. What behaviors helped to fuel those successes? Then list all the times you began to doubt yourself or your magick. Write out what was happening in those moments that made you feel defeated. Next, identify where you could use the successful tactics in place of the defeating feelings. As you move forward, refer to this journal entry to help encourage you forward as you manifest your intention.

The Little Things Matter

In life, everyone is faced with big issues. From job loss to serious trauma, no one is exempt from the harsh realities of life. How we deal with those moments is what defines us as people. The fact that most of us rarely completely give up is a testament to the idea that we are magickal beings even if we don't realize this to be our truth. We all put in the work necessary for success to some degree. While those degrees may vary widely, the fact remains that it is more often the case that we all persist.

In working magick, the idea that mundane things matter should come as no surprise. It is not common for anything in the world to be simply handed to us. Most of us are familiar with the idea that we have to work for what we want. In this way, it is the little things we do that help us reach our goals.

You might seek counselling to heal your mind so that you can trust a love when it enters your life. Or, like me, you could pursue the owner of a coffee shop for a minimum wage position to help make ends meet. These are examples of the steps we can take in order to reach our desired goals. They are things that must be done in order to manifest intentions. If magick takes energy from all sorts of correspondences, why wouldn't it also need us to exert energy in our everyday life?

It is the small things we do on a daily basis that transforms us into the people others respect. If you want a better position at work, you have to show your boss that you deserve it. The same holds true with princes and frogs, you'll have to kiss a few before you find the right one.

Magick will work; it does all the time. But it requires a sacrifice: time spent job hunting, dating, or saving money. It requires that you do the work, the stuff no one really wants to do. That's when you begin to see results. Spell work isn't always about the spell—sometimes it's about the mundane work as well.

Suggested Reading

Spells for Tough Times: Crafting Hope When Faced with Life's Thorniest Challenges by Kerri Connor. Llewellyn Publications, 2012.

The Little Work: Magick to Transform Your Everyday Life by Durgadas Allon Duriel. Llewellyn Publications, 2020.

Part Two
THE PILLARS OF WITCHCRAFT

In magick is a concept called the Four Pillars of Witchcraft. Not everyone lives by these pillars, but they make great sense to me. The idea is that together they comprise the structure that holds up Witchcraft. When you look at a building, you see walls and a roof. What you usually don't see is the foundation or the supports that tie the structure together.

Pillars can be made out of anything. In ancient days, temples were constructed with pillars of marble. In the present, you may find four-by-fours supporting the roof on your porch or concrete pylons holding up the decks of a parking garage. Basically, these are all pillars.

Like those of the ancient world or the ones in your home, the Pillars of Witchcraft help to support our magick, giving our spell craft the structure necessary to function in the way it is needed. In other words, these four principles help us perform magick that works.

The Four Pillars of Witchcraft are: to Keep Silent, to Dare, to Will, and to Know. All four concepts have equal importance. In this part of the book I dive deeply into each pillar with the goal of helping you to build upon the foundation laid out in part one.

7
To Keep Silent

I find that to be silent holds great power. I talk a lot, I don't always listen, I speak out of turn, and I don't keep secrets well. For these reasons I find myself practicing silence more often than anything else. The four pillars are like any other aspect of magick—they take a lot of work and daily effort.

In regard to silence, biting your tongue or keeping things from others is not all there is to this principle. Knowing when to speak and what to say is an important piece in understanding silence in our mundane lives that runs deeper in magick. To Keep Silent is not always about what you're not saying. You don't have to *be* silent in order to Keep Silent because this idea carries with it several other responsibilities.

Just as much as we have a right to our privacy, others have a right to not know the things that we should keep private— the first aspect of silence in the most literal sense. In relation to Witchcraft, not everyone needs to know that we are Witches. In truth, it is unlikely that most people even care what we are practicing. When it comes to relating to other people, keeping our ways of life to ourselves is a courtesy to the rest of our human family. This doesn't mean we can't live openly and be ourselves, it just means we should not impose our experiences on others.

Another aspect of this pillar is keeping things that you've done to yourself. When it comes to magick, it is important to keep other people out of our business. Unless we are performing a ritual with others, sharing is not required. We are often better off not telling anyone, including Witch friends, about the magick we create. Spell crafting is an intimate thing; inviting others into it should be done with the same level of discernment one would use for telling personal secrets. There are several reasons for keeping our workings to ourselves. The most imperative reason is that we ought not invite other people's energy into our spells. This can prove to be counterproductive and sometimes it could even undermine the magick we've performed.

A third facet to the pillar of silence is about listening instead of speaking. Witchcraft is the path of the wise. It is important to know when it is your turn to speak and when it is your turn to listen. Listening quietly can tell a Witch so much about others. Learning only happens when we shut down our ego and open our ears. Paying attention to what is being said in any situation is likely to lead to a greater understanding in general. A wise Witch knows the importance of understanding the whole circumstance as opposed to fragments colored with our own emotions and projected feelings. Taking the time to truly listen illuminates our path to power.

As a practice, keeping silent will not only help us gain insight into the world around us, it also will protect us from countless threats along the way. Knowing when to speak and what to say empowers us only if we choose to maintain our silence otherwise.

Finally, listening informs our power base so that we may rise up against any opposition that comes our way. There is a strength in silence that truly helps to maintain the structure of magick. Learning to keep silent will not only help us to be more adept humans but also stronger Witches as well.

My Story: No Use Explaining the Truth

I have had an aversion to Christianity since realizing I was gay. However, being homeless causes a person to reassess their opinions on things. For instance, when I saw a route out of my hardship, it was an easy choice to dive right in, regardless of my morals. This is how I became a "Christian" at eighteen.

I find Christians to be somewhat pious most of the time. I was shocked when I met some who weren't. They were a pretty cool couple I came across about a month into working at the coffee shop. They were young and married. She had that purple-ish white hair you see all the time now and his hair was blue. I didn't know they were Christians the first night they asked me if I needed a place to sleep. When we got to their house, they asked me if they could pray for me, and it became obvious. Although I was uncomfortable with the idea, I said yes anyway out of fear they'd rescind their offer for the night.

After that, the couple kept showing up. They'd offer me a place to sleep and dinner. He gave me clothes he didn't wear anymore, and she would do my laundry while preparing food. They told me if I ever had a night when I couldn't find a place to stay, I could just show up and they would let me in. It felt like a real friendship. They didn't want anything more than to save my soul. From my point of view, it seemed like a valid endeavor.

I stayed at their apartment often and eventually they told me they could help me more but I just needed to help myself. The couple believed that if I became a Christian, God would deliver me from the situation I was in. My first step was to accept Jesus as my savior. I was not prepared to do that. Everything I knew told me that this was not my path. I was honest with them. I told them I knew being gay was an issue for God and I couldn't change that about myself. They replied that they understood I felt as though I didn't have a choice in the matter. Their opinion was that the choice comes in not participating in the behavior. In other words, I could be gay as long as I abstained from sex completely for the rest of my life, which is what it would take for God to help me. As crazy as it seemed, it made some sense to me: they weren't exactly telling me not to like men, just that I couldn't have sex with them.

I toyed with the idea of trying to be a straight man. It seemed like things in my life would be easier if I could pull it off, but the trouble was I didn't think it was possible. Eventually, out of desperation, I told them I would try. If abstinence was "all" it would take, then it couldn't be that hard. What they didn't know wouldn't hurt them and would definitely help me. I kept silent about my sex life and they jumped into action, attempting to find me permanent shelter.

They introduced me to a guy who would let me live with him. I, of course, assumed he had ulterior motives. He introduced me to a church where the pastor's wife decided that she could convert me "back" to being straight. These people thought it was a choice to be gay, so there was no use explaining the truth to them.

The pastor's wife, two deacons, and their wives as well, met with me weekly. We would discuss my experiences with molestation and they would tell me this is when the demon entered my life. I was informed that I wasn't really gay—I was just possessed by a demon. I told them about being a prostitute and they told me this was how the demon kept me invested. Eventually we talked about the priest from my childhood and how I stopped going to church. It was their contention that Catholicism was not really Christianity but rather Witchcraft. This prompted me to tell them I had been a Witch, that I had the word tattooed to my back in Chinese. Again, their position was that this was the demon's work, not my own.

They prayed over me, pouring the fire of God into my soul to cleanse the demon from me. They watched to see if I would fall over when they put their hands on my head and speak in tongues. They hoped for some sort of confirmation of a miracle, that I would be suddenly healed of this affliction. I just sat there quietly. I let them lay hands on me and holler their incomprehensible words in my face. I held back giggles as their hands shook with conviction and I rested easy knowing that as long as they believed this was working, I had a place to sleep.

Eventually I moved in with the pastor, his wife, and their two kids; both kids were a little older than me, so it was basically a house full of adults. On the surface I was the picture of Christianity. I went to church twice a week and showed up to help the administration with random work when I was bored. I got a job and started thinking that I could have a normal life. I even considered going back to school so I could graduate.

Everything seemed perfect until it wasn't. Secrets aren't easy for me but I held tight to the lie that I was straight. At the time, AOL was a big deal. Being previously homeless, I wasn't exposed to the then-new phenomenon of chat rooms, though I was aware that there were chat rooms dedicated to man-on-man action. Late at night after everyone was asleep, I would sign on and talk to men. I felt relief in being able to be myself, even if it was hidden in an online persona. My ploy was flawless until the night the pastor's wife caught me in the chat room. Things went downhill from there.

The moment the Christians realized they didn't pray the gay away, that they couldn't rid me of this supposed demon, their whole demeanor changed. I was apologetic. I tried to cover with another lie, saying I was just ministering to men in the chat. I told them I was trying to convert others from a life of sin. No one believed me. I was no longer possessed by a demon; to them I *was* the demon. They turned their backs on me in a single heartbeat. Within weeks I was back on the streets, on my own.

If I Had Known

"Silence is golden" is a saying that gets thrown around a lot. The statement is full of sound reasoning but for a person like myself is a tall order. I want to share my life with others. I want to let people see behind the curtain we all seem to pull around our truths. And yet that desire has been my ruin more than a few times in life. Most people don't want the truth, not when it shatters their beliefs or proves to them there are weak spots in their foundation. Like the Christians from my past who threw me away when my truth came to light, it's common for people to want to discard anything contrary to the lies they tell themselves. This is why silence has power.

I needed the help of the Christians, and only keeping silent would have helped me protect myself in a hostile environment where I needed to lie as a means for survival. If they needed to continue to believe their conversion therapy was working, why wouldn't I have done all I could to play that part? In upholding my lie, I was saving myself. If I had known then that silence in this circumstance meant more than not speaking, the course of my life would have been dramatically different.

Much like most things in magick and Witchcraft, multiple meanings can be gleaned from the idea of silence. On the surface the word means "quiet"; to be silent is to not make a sound. But to Keep Silent holds more meaning. Keeping my secret protected meant to not act. It meant that in order to protect myself and my lie, I needed to do all I could to live up to the expectation that was put upon me. In order to maintain my safety, it was my duty to maintain the lie at all costs. This would have meant never getting online to chat with other gay men. Keeping silent in this way would have maintained my stability, but that wasn't healthy.

Silence for me should never have been about not being true to myself. Being a gay man is a big part of who I am as a human. While it doesn't define me as a person, my love for men is innate and intricately tied to everything else in my life. From my personality to how I communicate, my sexuality is as much a part of me as my own hand. When I made the choice to stifle that part of who I am, I amputated a piece of my being from itself.

At the time, this sort of silence made sense because it was out of an act of desperation that I quieted my sexuality. But no one should ever compromise who they are for the sake of a false sense of security. That's not really how the power of silence works. If I had known then that keeping silent meant discerning the situation better, I might have found a much more stable environment with which to shelter myself from the streets. I didn't understand silence at the time. I thought that lying about myself made me a stronger person for persevering despite my better judgment.

What I have learned since those days as a faux Christian is that silence would not have been lying about myself. Deceiving the Christians was like wrapping gauze on a wound that needed stitches. It didn't actually help me get further. My silence in this case only offered a temporary reprieve from a world I was thrown right back into the moment the mask of my lie fell away.

Silence means letting people talk their talk while gleaning the pieces of wisdom scattered within their bigotry. It means not accepting everything someone has to say but also not fighting against it either. None of us will ever be able to create a change in another person who is unwilling to see our truth. Just as the Christians could not convert my sexuality, I could not convert their beliefs into accepting me.

If I had understood silence at the time, I could have taken advantage of the cool-colored-hair couple to the point of learning how they survived. They were my age, worked in the service industry just as I did, and they were succeeding in sheltering themselves. Instead of engaging in conversations about God and how it could help me become a Christian, I could have directed the conversation toward being a responsible young adult.

I could have begun to build my own structure on top of the pillar of silence. By not giving too much information about myself, I would have side-stepped the conversion attempts. In not discussing their viewpoints of my supposed sin, I would have protected myself from the temptation of an easy out, one built on a lie. I might have identified my own way to salvation by listening to what constructive information they could offer.

The Magick of Silence

In magick, so many things correspond with something else. It makes sense that the pillars of Witchcraft would also be associated with other aspects of magick as well. Silence is like the earth.

While the material world makes plenty of noise consider for a moment a seed. Once planted a seed does not announce itself immediately. It takes its time. It grows discreetly from within the womb of the earth until it is ready to sprout. Even then, once it has begun its journey above ground, a sapling remains quiet, steadily growing until one day it is noticed. Magick works in this way as well.

When we set our intentions, there is no need to announce them to the world. We have planted our seed and only need to water it with the mundane behaviors necessary to help those intentions grow. The magick is in our cultivation, which is not the words we have spoken but rather the actions we take to see our harvest come into fruition.

The more we speak about our intentions, the more likely we are to weaken our magick. What I mean is that if one were to cast a spell and then post it all over social media, it is more likely to falter or fail. Here's why: if a spell is like a seed, then the energy placed into your intention is like the water it needs to grow. If you are like me, you might have firsthand experience with what happens when you give a plant too much water—the plant dies.

When manifesting using magick, it is important to be aware that there is a delicate balance of energy needed to nourish our desires. Too much attention and the spells fail; too little and we are met with the same outcome. To Keep Silent is one way to help maintain the balance that allows our spells to flourish.

TRY THIS
Keys Are the Seeds

In this spell we tap into the idea of the silent seed growing. This is a simple working in which you plant your intentions and then watch them silently grow.

What You'll Need
- A set of keys, because they open doors
- Paper and something to write your intention with
- A place to dig a hole, as seeds must be planted
- A green candle and something to carve it with (green symbolizes growth)

The Process
On the candle, carve your intention into the wax. While you do this, envision it growing like a seed out of the ground. As you do this, see your goal becoming actualized. Picture what your life will be like once your goal is achieved. Then on a new moon, place your energy into the candle by holding it in your hands and pushing your intentions into it. Once you've finished with the candle, dig a hole. It does not have to be very deep, but it should be deep enough to bury the keys you have brought with you. Place the candle in the hole and light it. Sit in stillness and watch the candle burn. As the wax melts, envision your intention entering the soil. See the wax become one with the dirt, all the while envisioning the wax as the fertilizer that will feed your intention once planted into the earth.

Wrap the keys in a piece of paper on which you have written your intention. This is now your seed. Plant the metaphoric seed and walk away. Your intention will grow from the soil and become manifest. Never speak of the magick you performed. Allow your intention to grow organically.

Communication Without Words

Of all the deities I've ever learned about, none stand out so boldly in regard to communication as Hermes. While there are several other aspects to this god of the Greek pantheon, the role he plays as the messenger, in my opinion, is the most vital. Consider for a moment how often a message is received through our clairsenses. The instances when you know that the information you are obtaining from the Source is a literal communication meant just for you to decipher. Whether you work with this deity or not, the importance of the message you receive in these moments holds power. It is easy to understand that these communications are delivered via some sort of divinity.

Just as Hermes is multifaceted in his godliness, so too is communication diverse in the way it plays out in our lives. It's no stretch of the imagination to identify that silence is a form of communication as well. Consider a moment how loudly the message is received when you give or are given the silent treatment. When applied correctly, silence can be deafening.

Not speaking or not saying anything can hold more power and take down larger ramparts than the trumpets of biblical Jericho. Silence holds power because it is what you are *not* saying that can suck the confidence out of a person. But it is also in silence that what you are not saying can grow to become a message of truth and clarity. It may be cliché, but actions really do speak louder than words. And the act of silence communicates so much more than nothing.

Using silence, we can tell someone that we will not stand for their behavior. We can say, "You don't deserve my time or attention." Silence can also tell somebody how much we care. Because I talk so often, if I am standing in silence with anyone who knows me, they are aware that my silence is stoic and respectful.

Breaking our silence can speak volumes as well. Knowing when to speak up and say, "That is enough, and now you will hear me" only holds power if we have kept our silence. To Keep Silent is magick because there is power in the dynamics of it. On each end of the spectrum, silence makes a statement. It communicates loud and clear through actions, just as Hermes did when he was only a child. From stealing cattle to creating the lyre, Hermes communicated his genius through actions, not words.

Learning to define our power as Witches through silence or the lack thereof builds a structure. Honing our skills in discerning when to best use this pillar of magick creates a stronger practice. When we learn how to communicate through silence, we learn how to speak like the Source.

TRY THIS
Help Me, Hermes

This is a candle spell for assistance in communication. Whether you are seeking messages from the Source or just trying to help a loved one understand you better, this spell will come in handy.

What You'll Need
- An orange candle, orange is the color of communication
- A yellow candle, yellow is the color of intellect
- Mustard seed powder, a spice that brings good luck and protection. It is often associated with Hermes.

- Star anise, another spice also associated with the god Hermes. It corresponds with blessings and protection. Additionally, star anise can be used to entice spirits to aid you in your spell work.

- Cinnamon, for healing, protection, and purification. This spice is known for giving magick a boost and for helping spell work manifest quickly.

- Frankincense, a resin that attracts peace and harmony as well as protection, strength, success, and prosperity. Frankincense has been used as an offering, to cleanse a space, and to empower magickal workings.

- Basil, an herb that corresponds with protection, peace, happiness, tranquility, and purification.

- Ginger powder, a spice that is well known for its protective properties.

- Orange peel, a citrusy herb that calls forth luck and happiness.

Preparations

Roll your candles through olive oil then stand them up so the excess oil can run off. After grinding your frankincense and star anise, shred your basil. Lay the three ingredients on a flat surface with the three powdered spices and the orange peel. Mix the seven magickal elements together while envisioning your intention. Put your energy into the herbs as you swirl your finger through the mixture. Finally, roll the candles in it. Stand the candles up and let them dry.

The Process

On a Wednesday (the day of Hermes), take your candles to a quiet place. Set one on your left side and one on your right. It doesn't matter which is where. The idea is only that you are in the center of the two. As you light your candles, call out to Hermes and ask him to assist you with your intentions on communication. Whether you are seeking messages from the Source or trying to express ideas or feelings in the physical world, be sure to make your petition clear.

Sit between the two candles until they have finished burning. While you are there, meditate on your petition and the best ways to bring your intentions into fruition.

Silence Is a Two-Way Street

When it comes to talking about magick, it is important to *not* do so. In a world with a growing interest in Witchcraft, one would think we could trust most people who similarly identify as Witches. Unfortunately, this is not the case. Magick works under the cloak of silence because other people can affect your spells with their own intentions. It is one thing to share your faith with a friend, but it is a wholly different thing to give them the ins and outs of every ritual or spell you perform. When I discuss my magick with anyone, it is typically someone I trust, and even then I only give enough information so that my intention and process remain a secret.

I love my sister dearly. She is also a practicing Witch, so we are able to discuss magick together often. Regardless of how much we share with each other, neither of us have ever divulged our spell work to the other. We spend a lot of our time talking about different things we've learned. Sometimes one of us might ask the other to consult on a plan we have for a spell, but we almost never give all the details. This is because we don't practice in the same ways. The path my sister walks is vastly different from mine. Either of us sharing all our details and plans would cause the other to chime in. We both have the best intentions for each other, but in the end her magick isn't mine to weigh in on and vice versa.

To Keep Silent means to discern what to share with others. People put power into our magick all the time with their beliefs. It is normally unintentional, but everyone has feelings and opinions. Sharing information about your spell work with someone could cause them to affect it negatively, even if they don't mean to. Imagine if you have a friend who is always down on their luck and you have constant prosperity. When you talk to them about the magick you perform in order to maintain that prosperity, it is very possible that they feel some form of resentment, even if they aren't aware of it. Their jealousy or longing for what you've got places undue strain on your magick, surrounding it with a negative force that could work against you.

When sharing with anyone, we are inviting them into our circle. We don't only invite their joy but also their other, less positive emotions. If we aren't careful, those negative emotions could cause our magick to falter or fail altogether. Friends tend to want the best for us, but it is also often the case that they will envy what we have, even when they are happy for us. Our friends likely don't want to send negative energy in our direction but they might on the level of the subconscious. That kind of energy can harm what could've been our best outcome significantly. For that reason, being aware of other's situations is a vital aspect to practicing silence.

Keeping silent about the work we do allows us to control the energy that goes into our magick. We navigate around energies all the time as we create the outcomes for our endeavors. Not sharing the details of our practice or intentions helps to maintain boundaries. Both well intentioned and unintentional input affect our spells. Why would we want to add more potential obstacles?

To Keep Silent is both a Witch's tool and responsibility. As a tool, silence allows us to protect our magick from unintentional gatekeeping. It also protects our spells from the influence of energies we don't want in the mix. As a responsibility, we are meant to remain silent so that we don't become gatekeepers ourselves. The power behind the pillar of silence is a two-way street; we don't want anyone influencing our spells any more than we want to alter the results for someone else. As long as we are vigilant in our silence we are likely to increase good outcomes for all involved.

Silence Is Stillness

Taking the time to rest in quietness is an imperative part of keeping silence. We all have busy days no matter what they consist of. Whether you're running around or dealing with family or work, I think most of us are hard pressed to find truly quiet moments.

There is a peace in silence, and too often we tend to try and fill silence with as much noise as we can. We default to music on the radio or conversations on the phone to fend off the quiet. We fill potentially peaceful moments with social media, books, or our own racing mind. You probably thought you were attaining silence when you sat down to scroll Facebook or Instagram. Maybe you thought there was peace in that great book you're reading right now. The truth is, this is not silence.

Silence is stillness; it is a distraction-free moment. Short of plugging our ears we would be hard pressed to find true silence anywhere in the world. There could be rain pounding on your tin roof, or an ocean outside your back door. Even in the middle of nowhere, the wind could be howling through trees, birds could be singing, or insects could be buzzing about. These are not sounds that negate silence; that is not the type of silence I am writing about.

The quiet I am referring to is that of our minds. Many people find this in meditation. Time constraints and a racing mind are among the most common reasons people often think they can't meditate. For a long time, I was guilty of using both these excuses. I've always had a mind like a whack-a-mole game. When I am able to rid myself of one thought, it is always replaced by another one. These additional thoughts show up in some other part of my mind. It literally feels like I am constantly chasing complete stillness. Because of this, I figured I could never meditate. Many of you probably have had this feeling as well. I've learned that it's okay to feel this way *and* it doesn't mean meditation is unattainable for us.

Meditation is like DNA or a snowflake—it looks different for everyone. I don't sit still and swipe all my thoughts away. I don't listen to a nice voice gently leading me through some sort of mind clearing; that sort of thing just puts me to sleep. For me, meditation is my drive home. I turn the radio off. I know the way because I've driven it a million times, so I don't have to actively think about what I am physically doing aside from paying some attention to the road ahead of me. I let thoughts happen; a million things go through my head. I acknowledge them and let them pass. Eventually, all the thoughts work themselves out and I reach a place where there aren't new ones coming in. I don't focus on not thinking, and I don't hone in on the details of my thoughts either.

What I do is allow a thought to come in. I don't analyze where it came from or how I feel about it. I look at it like I would graffiti on a passing train. I see the colors and the details. As long as I don't run along with the train, the words are gone before I can even recognize them. Everything becomes silent because eventually, all the train cars pass by. This creates mindfulness. Once all the racing thoughts are gone, I am in the moment. All that exists is me and the random scenery I pass on my drive home.

For many Witches, it is integral to be in touch with themselves. Becoming mindful in the moment is an excellent way to reach this state of being. In order to manifest anything, we have to know where our minds are. We have to be in the moment. If we aren't, our magick becomes influenced by things that don't pertain to our goals. You don't want to catch yourself thinking about the water bill while petitioning the Source for something completely unrelated. What you want is to be present, clear about your desires, and unencumbered by extraneous external distractions.

Mindfulness takes practice. It won't look the same for everyone, but seeking out silence is essential to developing as Witches.

TRY THIS
Becoming Mindful

Doing this once or twice a day will help to train you to control the thoughts that enter your mind while you are attempting to focus on something else. This is a great daily practice to participate in so that you can train yourself in being in the moment.

What You'll Need
- A quiet place
- A timer

The Process

Set your timer for ten minutes. Sit up straight but comfortably in a quiet place. Your shoulders and head should be relaxed but not slumped forward.

Close your eyes and begin to breathe deeply. Pay attention to how your chest rises and falls, how your belly expands and contracts with each breath. Visualize every inhale filling your body from head to toe. Then see it all leave as you exhale. Place all your focus into your breathing. When thoughts enter your mind, don't pay them any attention. Acknowledge that there is a thought but draw your focus back to your breath. If it helps you to maintain focus, count your inhales. Until the timer goes off, think only of your breathing.

Stop Speaking and Start Listening

It is only when we are quiet that we are able to truly hear anything. This is why magick can be created in silence. To maintain mindfulness we quiet our minds, and in order to understand the physical world around us, we must quiet our voices. When we stop speaking and start listening, we gain power in the knowledge we obtain.

Listening to background noise informs us of what is happening in our general vicinity. Sirens from emergency vehicles alert us to potential danger. When our dog barks, it could mean that someone is at the front door. And the subtle differences in a baby's cry can tell us what the infant needs. But listening can help us understand so much more than these mundane things. Listening can help us discern a person's true intentions.

There are people in the world who love to hear themselves talk. Whether they are right or wrong, they'll argue. Or maybe they will go on and on about a subject no one cares to hear about. Sometimes these types of people will start throwing out words no one knows, almost as if they are trying to assert that they are smarter than everyone else. To keep silent is to allow this to happen. Whether we want to hear them or not, listening to these sorts of people gives us an upper hand we would not obtain otherwise. I'm not telling you to suffer a toxic, holier-than-thou fool, but give them their space. Allow them to serve their purpose—sometimes it is in our best interest to let them do so. What they have to say may seem convoluted and trivial but what comes through might lead to a higher understanding of why they behave the way that they do.

Listening to hear what a person is really saying deep down under the surface of their words teaches us their true nature. It helps us to see through the facade they present to the world and gives us insight into what is happening in their minds. For example, you might learn that your boss's arrogance comes from a need to prove themselves. Understanding the people we share this world with will help us to navigate our surroundings with much more purpose and clarity.

If we take the time to listen to what those people are telling us with their behavior, we are likely to begin to understand how to shield ourselves from their energy. When we listen instead of speak, we learn how to develop a system of magick that works in our daily lives.

Continuing the earlier example, realizing the reason behind the arrogance of our boss helps us to not take it personally. We are then able to step outside of the situation and think with a clear mind on how best to combat the repercussions of their behavior. Perhaps carrying obsidian into work every day would help to absorb their negativity, but now with our knowledge gained from just listening, we can zero in on our boss's specific energy. Instead of absorbing the general negativity around us, we can focus our stone to do a specific job. This frees us from at least one major source of energy that could affect us, thus allowing room for the further development of protection in other areas at work.

Life isn't easy for anyone. Until we stop to listen, to understand the struggles of the people around us, we can't help ourselves deal. When we listen in order to understand, things become much more manageable. In this way, listening becomes a super power, an advantage against most of the world.

TRY THIS
Don't Speak

Spend one day not saying anything. Unless it is vital that you must talk, do not speak to another person. Don't speak out loud to yourself either. Take a solid twenty-four hours and just listen to what everyone else has to say. Listen to the sounds of the earth as well. Couple this exercise with the journal prompt that follows.

JOURNAL PROMPT
What Did You Hear?

After spending the day just listening to people and the world around you, what sort of messages rang clear? Did you learn more about a person? Your environment? Have you gained an understanding of why someone behaves the way they do? Do you understand your surroundings?

Write down all the insight you obtained from quieting yourself enough to pay attention to the world you exist in.

Silence Is Your Savior

In recent years the term and idea of "coming out of the broom closet" has become popular, which is when a Witch begins to become public about who they are spiritually. Just the idea that a term like this exists is evidence that there still is a lack of acceptance for our way of life. People appear to be accepting of us today, but this doesn't mean they always are.

For a moment, I want you to picture yourself in the seventeenth century. Isaac Newton is only a child, so the world isn't even aware that there are laws of physics yet. Living in Europe, you have grown up learning all about herbs and the forest. Through mom and maybe even dad, you have quite a lot of knowledge about healing with elements of the earth. In the modern world, we may call this holistic or natural, but back then, this was Witchcraft.

It is a time of fear for many because Matthew Hopkins is running around "identifying Witches." This fool is noted as being the Witchfinder General in a book called *The Discovery of Witches* written in 1647. Matty and his bros are going from town to town, stripping women and searching for birthmarks and extra nipples. This, they contend, is the Devil's mark and a sure sign of being a Witch. They are strapping supposed Witches to chairs and throwing them in water to see if they float. Those who sink are innocent but also they are dead.

Now keep imagining this is your world. There's no internet or true education. Most people believe in Christianity, and it's a real possibility that if offended, someone may start hollering that you are a Witch. The problem is that most of the people accused of Witchcraft are very likely not Witches, but you in this instance actually are. Back then, in the seventeenth century, silence was your savior.

Fast forward to now, past the Industrial Revolution, past the beginning of the feminist movement. Fast forward to today where in America and most European countries, you can be almost anything and for the most part safely live your truth. Silence as a Witch means a completely different thing as compared to the seventeenth century. We live in a period of time when many of us can live out loud. And while not everyone everywhere is safe from everything, there are a lot of safe spaces for you to be yourself depending on what country you live in.

It isn't hard to search for podcasts about being a Witch. You can join groups on Facebook to learn about Witchcraft. The hashtag #Witch populates a ton of results on Instagram. And YouTube is full of videos on the topic as well. Many times, it is safer today to be a Witch than it is to have a brown shade of skin in America.

Silence alone will protect you in our Christian dominated world. Sharing with people that you are a Witch is likely to come with a dynamic set of reactions. Some may be completely accepting while others may only *appear* to accept you. The reverse could happen as well. From being told you're evil to requests that you prove your status, opposition is still prevalent. In the end, we have no control over how people react to us. This is why to Keep Silent is so important.

Just like when I was forced to deny my own sexuality, many Witches are forced to hide who they are even now. While I was homeless, I thought I was receiving help regardless of who I truly was. When the other shoe dropped, I was locked in a trap that left me feeling as if I was required to change in order to receive the help I needed. We all have people like this in our lives, people who seem to care about us on the surface as long as we live up to their expectations. The moment they realize we don't, their feelings change.

Silence as a way to protect ourselves is an old idea that persists in the modern world. Sharing with others that we are Witches could create problems in our professional, social, and home lives. While it would be great if we were able to live out loud, it is not always the case. Many of us are forced into situations where we depend on a person or circumstance in order to survive. Being open about our magick could cause our downfall. Although radical acceptance is growing in today's world, it may not always be this way. For now, knowing when to share our Witchcraft with others is imperative for the well-being of many Witches worldwide.

Thankfully we aren't living in the dark ages. The term "Witch hunt" is now more likely to be used by a white man under public scrutiny for misbehavior than it is to be related to anything remotely Witchcraft related. Regardless, discernment is necessary when outing ourselves as Witches. In a world where being a professional Witch is a real thing, it can become tempting to let anyone and everyone know our spiritual alignment. It is easy for a Christian to discuss their god on national television, but it is important to remember that when a true Witch does this very same thing, they are likely to receive death threats for being open about who they are.

Protecting ourselves from bigotry and discrimination is not shameful—it is necessary. Allowing the shroud of silence to keep us safe is one thing that Witches have had to do for a long time. Our ancestors didn't have the safe spaces that blogs and social media provide for us. Keeping silent for them held power because it was under the protective shadow of silence where they found comfort in who they were. I want nothing more than for all of us to be in a situation where we can shout from the rooftops that we are Witches. I want everyone to have the public life many of those who are not Witches are afforded. But I don't want any of it at the cost of safety, sanity, or well-being. Absolutely every one of us deserves to live out loud. If that sort of life could create catastrophic situations though, it would be best to protect yourself in keeping silent about who you are, at least while it is necessary.

TRY THIS
Create an Alternative

If you must live in the broom closet, this exercise is for you.

What You'll Need
- Internet
- A social media presence
- A witty pseudonym

The Process
With the rise of social media, it isn't uncommon to have more than one profile on several different platforms. Build a profile you can use to live your Witchcraft life out loud. Do this with discernment and from a place of protection. If you cannot live completely out of the broom closet, create a digital persona who can.

Be honest and true to yourself when you create this alternative with the understanding that you are allowing yourself to experience the freedom that living in the twenty-first century offers.

Holding Up the Structure

Silence is powerful—it holds up the structure of Witchcraft and works in concert with the other pillars in order to help us create our magick. From understanding our world because we listen to protecting us through not giving away too much information on ourselves or our spells, silence is worth keeping. All the pillars of magick are vital for our spell crafting lives, but silence is the first because its power is so profoundly dynamic.

Safety, protected spells, informed lives, and mindfulness are things no Witch should go without. The level of power just one aspect of silence can provide is amazing, but enveloping ourselves in every facet of this pillar is sure to level up a Witch's practice. We are capable of so much when we find the resources to tap into and use them to create the life we want to live. Silence isn't an unattainable goal for any of us. Instead, it is an innate part of all of us. We only need to choose to access this piece of ourselves in order to help us manifest our desires.

Through stillness, we are able to know our truths. In listening, we can understand our surroundings. With discernment, we are able to protect not only our wellbeing but also our magick. When it comes to the pillar that is To Keep Silent, it is clear that upholding this idea is essential to crafting true magick that works. In remaining silent, we are able to develop deeper magick that isn't dependent on spells and rituals. We hold ourselves up through a sense of daring to keep silent that which would help us see our goals come to light.

Suggested Reading

A Witch's Book of Silence by Karina BlackHeart. Kbh Enterprises, 2015.

8
To Dare

*Y*ou are magick. No matter who you are or where you're from, I know this to be true. You may not be a Witch, yet there is a deep-seated magickal part of you that shines through, even if only in small amounts. Our true essence is like a light that cannot be contained. It finds its way out into the world regardless of our efforts to suppress it. Who we are at our core, no matter what that might be, cannot be hidden. Choosing to embrace those pieces of who we are is to Dare.

A dare is a challenge, especially one that proves courage or defies something. When you are daring to do something you're using all of your bravery. Worries are cast aside despite your fears; doing something *even though* it is an act of daring. That is why it holds power. The second pillar of Witchcraft is to Dare, an idea that applies to the other three pillars: you can dare to Be Silent, you can dare to Will, and you can dare to Know. There is a strength in daring that resonates with the power of a pillar that supports a building.

Think about how scared you were the first time you had to stand in front of a group and talk. Think about how anxious you were when you went to your first day of school. How much fear did you fight back when you took the chance and loved for the first time? How worried were you when you came out of the closet to your parents? Also think about how unsure of yourself you were when you took that job with no experience. You made it, though, didn't you? Things worked out one way or another and you survived whether the outcome was good or bad. You dared to do the thing despite your fear, anxiety, worry, and whatever else.

To Dare is to summon all your power into doing the thing regardless of trepidation, which is why it's a pillar and how it holds magick up: daring is our inner strength. When we look at the big picture, we can see that daring is multifaceted. To Dare is to be yourself, to love and listen to yourself, to go boldly into the unknown, to cut your own path through life, and to let go of what doesn't serve you. To Dare is to stand up in the face of danger or tragedy and say, "Nope, you're not getting me."

In practicing magick we are daring in one way or another. We dare to believe in ourselves and our magick, or to take a chance on the unknown. We dare to defy obstacles and to listen to ourselves first, to love ourselves, or to work on the parts of us that need some improvement. When we practice magick, we are daring to make a change that is more often than not started within ourselves.

My Story: Not Like This

I've suffered through bouts of clinical depression, especially during the years I spent homeless, a normal thing for any human. Too often we as a society want to cover up the fact that many of us struggle through mental health issues. We are often left to assume we are alone in these illnesses, but the facts are that more of us are dealing with it than we may think. What matters is that despite my depression while surviving on the streets, I continued forward.

I don't like to drink alcohol much, but while homeless in Summerville, South Carolina, I became old enough to buy it. This was a small town, vastly different from Dallas. The friends I had would help me find places to sleep as best they could, but by and large I was alone. Never mind that I followed a boy to Summerville. He was no help at all. We became friends in Kentucky while we both attended Job Corps training. I was meant to learn a trade while I was there but that got me nowhere.

Summerville didn't have much. When I couldn't spend the night indoors anywhere, I might be found sleeping in a broken-down car in a friend's backyard. When her father put a stop to that, I had to find shelter in other ways. I got lucky for a few clear nights because someone had donated a couch to the Goodwill store. Sitting outside on the loading dock for days, this couch made a perfect bed until it rained.

In order to stay dry, I found myself under a bridge. I was the troll of Summerville for a week while it rained nonstop. It was under this bridge I first learned just how daring I was.

I had nothing—no money, no job, and nowhere comfortable to sleep once that couch was soaked. I was under a bridge and the feeling of loss really set in. I thought I had friends and that I was going to be stable after the Job Corps, but that's nowhere near how things turned out. There was no recourse and I had lost my will. What would you do?

I thought it was time to end it. I took my belt off that day and took the time to punch a new hole in it. The new hole was meant to ensure the belt would choke me when I wrapped it around my neck. I tightened the belt until I couldn't breathe. The world became black in my peripheral vision. My face grew tight. My mind raced with all the things I thought I might have done but hadn't. At that moment, I heard myself, my true self. That part of me that hadn't yet had the chance to shine slapped myself in the face and said, "Not like this." As the world darkened around me, I could hear the blood in my head struggling to circulate past the belt around my neck. I released it. I let go of my failure as the belt was loosened.

I didn't know where to go, but I knew I was done under the bridge. I was daring myself to live. I walked up the road to where I'd had my septum pierced months earlier. In addition to a piercing parlor, it was also a metaphysical shop. The rain stopped while I was in the shop. The owners of the store were cool. I stood there and talked to them for a while. It was okay that I just hung out for a bit. I asked them about work but they had none to offer. I told them about the struggle that was my life at the moment. And then they offered me a place to stay.

If I Had Known

When I look back at that moment under the bridge in Summerville, it seems so clear that choosing to loosen the belt from my neck was daring. I wanted to die but I stopped. I honestly thought at the time that I was being a coward, that I just couldn't go through with killing myself. But the truth is that I chose to keep going. The truth is that I dared to face my problems and to find a constructive way out of them. If only I had known that the magick of daring to defy a circumstance would be reciprocated with rewards, I would have immediately changed my life moving forward.

To Dare means to believe in the unbelievable, to put faith into something even though the evidence for that faith doesn't exist. When I dared to keep living, to climb out from under that bridge, I made a choice to put faith into the idea that things could still get better. Up until that moment, I had no reason to trust this would be the case. But when I believed anyway, I was given the proof I needed. At the time, I didn't know that daring was a thing. I was just instinctually doing it.

Witchcraft works in this same way sometimes; it doesn't always take spells and obvious intentions. Sometimes it's just something we manifest without knowing. That day, I decided not to give up. I decided to live regardless of my situation. I dared to see what would happen next. And what happened was Witches took me in.

Magick defies the odds. It creates doorways for us where there were once just walls. When we use magick, we are required to believe that the work we are doing can create change. It becomes necessary for us to believe in the unbelievable. To Dare, to do something even though all the evidence tells us it can't be done is magick by itself. Then, when the impossible becomes possible, it seems clear that our faith in the matter is what fueled the manifestation of our desires.

I chose to go forward into the unknown without the certainty that anything would change for the better. I decided to fight for me, to listen to myself and know that the voice in my mind was right. I was not meant to be found dead under a bridge in some small town in South Carolina. I was meant to go into the world and overcome every obstacle placed before me. This life I was living was my hero's journey. And what is a hero if not daring?

What I didn't know then was that belief is a key tenant to performing magick. If I wasn't daring enough to put faith in my intentions, how could I expect the Source to provide for me? Manifesting anything requires an unwavering sense of knowing that you can attain what you are endeavoring to accomplish. Rest assured you are daring to do just that when you lack the empirical evidence that tells you it is possible.

The fear, loneliness, and pain of being homeless were the trials that would help me become the Witch I am today. Just as I had learned the power of silence in Dallas, in Summerville I was learning the strength bestowed by daring. I had nothing, but I dared to continue. I loved myself regardless of my situation. I chose to let go of the fear and instead dared to hope for something better.

If I had known that daring to believe in myself would have led me to where I am today; I wouldn't have been daring to do anything. It was only through pushing forward, regardless of the fact that the odds were not in my favor, that I earned the knowledge I now possess. To Dare is to wield power even if you feel powerless because when you dare, you beat the odds in the belief that nothing can stop you.

Daring to Be Magick

When it comes to practicing magick, it isn't easy to enumerate the steps one ought to take while manifesting. A single practitioner is likely to take a different series of steps depending on their goal. There is one safe bet, though: a Witch must believe that they can do the magick well before performing any spells or rituals. To believe in ourselves is to be daring, which is why to Dare is a pillar of Witchcraft.

To Dare is connected to the element of water. This isn't really a surprise when you think about it. Water has the power to carve canyons into the earth. It has the audacity to rush over boulders standing in its way and pool at the bottom of a cliff side it has just fallen over. Water finds its path. It dares to go where it chooses and remains unencumbered by anything that stands in its way. Although not sentient as far as we know, water is daring nonetheless. It moves forward as if striving to collate with itself, becoming something larger like a lake or the ocean. More often than not, water succeeds.

When casting a spell, it is as if we embrace the spirit of water, daring to defy the circumstances we face. Like water, a Witch finds their path and follows it regardless of the obstacles that stand in their way. They set their intention as if endeavoring to reach the ocean. Whether babbling like a brook or rushing like a river, a Witch moves forward. And when they fall, they gather themselves and then they keep going. This is daring to be magick.

When we know we are magick and dare to believe in ourselves, we become a force of nature. Daring to face our obstacles head on feeds our power because it informs us that we can face the next set of them as well. Like the river moving past a boulder only to crash into the next one, so too do we move forward.

TRY THIS
Be the Body of Water

In this exercise you are connecting to the element of water. This is a practice meant to help you relax and become one with your surroundings. Since more than half of our own bodies are made of water, this should feel pretty natural to most people. A caveat: Do not try this if you are sleepy or drowsy. The risk of drowning is real, and you should be as alert as possible in order to protect your own safety.

What You'll Need
- A shower, pool, lake, river, ocean, or bathtub

The Process

Enter a body of water. If this is a shower, sit on the floor and let the water pour over you. In a larger body of water or a tub, keep your head above the water but your torso submerged.

From your heart center, reach out with your energy. Let it spread across the surface of the water. Feel as it becomes one with every drop, wave, or ripple around you. Stay in this moment. Feel the familiarity of water and know that your body knows it is as much a part of the cycle as anything else.

Move on to the journal prompt that follows.

JOURNAL PROMPT
In Consideration of Water

Consider where the water you were one with; where has it been? Was it once a glacier? Did it flow down a mountain or was it poured into a lake from a recent storm? Did it travel through pipes to get to you? Was it from a well? Has this water touched every continent and island on earth? Think about the journey that water has taken. How can you relate? What trials must water overcome to reach this place you submerged yourself in?

Write down the characteristics about water that resonate with you. In what way are you like the water you were one with?

Overcoming Obstacles

The human condition is lousy with trials and tribulations. Whether we are dealing with finances, health issues, or anything else, the struggle for all of us is real. Even the mundane people of the world dare to persist regardless of whatever is facing them. As Witches, we can use magick to gain the upper hand. Our obstacles are no more or less daunting than anyone else's. Even with spell casting on our side, we may encounter situations that require more from us than we think we can handle. Petitioning the help of a deity in these moments can often help to alleviate the stress these circumstances might present.

In the Hindu pantheon is a god well-suited for moments like these. Ganesha is known for many things. Usually featured with the head of an elephant and the four armed body of a man with a pot belly, this deity is considered the god of beginnings as well as wisdom. He is typically honored first in most Hindu practices, and he can be commonly found adorning the main entrance to many houses. But the stand out attribution of this god is his assistance in overcoming obstacles.

Many of the myths about Ganesha depict him as not only dealing with issues through wisdom and ingenuity but also as being daring while doing so. When we are faced with the problems life presents to all of us, it is important to approach those moments in the same way. While it is unlikely we would seal our bellies with the body of a snake were it to burst open, it would not be unusual for a Witch to come up with a magickal fix for a mundane obstacle.

There is almost always more than one way to handle a situation that creates a roadblock in our path. Turning to magick in these moments is one surefire way to fight back. Imagine the fear a child god like Ganesha felt when Shiva demanded access to the bathing Parvati. And yet, he stood his ground … only to have his head cut off and replaced with an elephant's. Like a Witch casting a spell to face their troubles, Ganesha stood up against his adversary in the moment.

In magick, we are often faced with a test of our own ability to be daring. But upon standing our ground and believing in ourselves, we are ultimately rewarded. Much like Ganesha stands out from his pantheon for having the head of an elephant, we stand out amongst our contemporaries when we dare to face our trials. In the end, the reward for making it to the other side of our tribulations often garners us more respect than we initially had.

TRY THIS
Removing Obstacles with Ganesha

What follows is a mantra to Lord Ganesha. If the words seem difficult, a simple internet search will set you on the path to proper pronunciation. Do this practice for at least a week, although it certainly wouldn't hurt to start each day with the intention of removing obstacles.

What You'll Need
- The words
- A safe quiet place
- A white candle

The Words
- Om: The sound of the vibration of the universe. It opens the mantra.
- Gam: The sound of Ganesha

- Ganapataye: Another name for Ganesha, who removes obstacles
- Namaha: A respectful greeting that says, "I honor you"

Put together, the four words basically say: "Hey there, Ganesha. I am here and I am honoring you. Can I have a little help?"

The Process

Sit in a quiet place and light your candle. If you are using a large candle you can mark it evenly a few times. This will act like a timer. In the Hindu religion this mantra is typically repeated 108 times but timing it with a candle to focus on is the way I have always practiced this mantra. You can sing the mantra or just repeat it. While you are chanting the mantra visualize your obstacles for the day being removed. Focus on the peace you feel from not being weighed down by your troubles.

Be the Fool

In tarot, the Fool carries with it the number zero—it is neither at the end nor the beginning of the major arcana. Instead, this card is the whole journey of human existence. The Fool is daring, taking a chance no matter what the outcome may be. The depiction is almost always of a person walking along with all their belongings slung over their shoulder. Typically the figure has an expression of serenity or carelessness on their face. And normally the figure is approaching a cliff. This person doesn't know what is coming next, and the magickal meaning of this card is that it doesn't matter—the point is the courage to take the journey.

The fool approaches a ledge. The pathway up ahead is blocked as far as we can tell, yet still they press on, ready to face whatever may come. Who knows what's just beyond that cliff? We the viewers can't see what is coming, and the fool themselves is seemingly unaware that the cliff is even there. And yet, they continue forward into the unknown. The fool is taking the chance.

Too often the term *fool* carries a negative connotation, usually meaning someone is being silly or idiotic. There is no respect present in referring to a person as a fool. However, when this tarot card is pulled, we are often encouraged by its appearance. To be unwitting or to make foolhardy decisions is something society wants us to shy away from. We are expected to have all of our steps planned out ahead of time. We are expected to know what is beyond the cliff ahead of us. The idea behind this major arcana card tells us the opposite. It tells us to go out and be daring, to take the path ahead despite not knowing.

To Dare is to be the Fool of the Tarot. This pillar of Witchcraft asks us to allow the road to roll out ahead of us. It asks us to trust our path regardless of what we can and cannot see along the way. The bravery required in daring is where the magick of this pillar comes into action. If I had not dared to continue that day under the bridge in Summerville, if I had let that be the end of my story, this dream to write a book would never have come into fruition. That day was my cliff. I was standing on the ledge, ready to give up, to call it quits, to die. But my inner strength knew better. For me, I saw no path forward, only a cliff. Choosing to live became a leap of faith.

As humans we come into these sorts of moments all the time. We find ourselves facing the unknown and we are forced to make the choice whether or not we will dare to move forward or stop dead in our tracks. It is imperative that we embody the idea of the Fool who is walking through a mountainous trail. If we are daring enough to not fear the terrain we find ourselves in, we are likely to find our way through it. For all anyone knows, there is a ledge under the cliff the Fool is approaching. It could be that this ledge leads to a higher elevation. The power the Fool reminds us of is this: even if we find ourselves in an uncomfortable situation, we have the ability to make the best of it. We have all that we need; it is up to us to trust the process and continue forward regardless of the present state we find ourselves in.

To Dare is to be brave, to go forward in trust that our outcomes will meet our needs. A leap of faith is required when we are practicing our magick, because manifestation often comes through in unlikely ways. What we expect is not always what we receive, but when we pay close attention, it is easy to see that we obtain all that we require to get through our journeys. Our intuition is a gift; when we dare to trust it despite the evidence of our current circumstances we will find that we have risen rather than fallen off of the cliff.

JOURNAL PROMPT
What Chances Can You Take?

Sit with your journal and consider for a moment how you could let go of control for a moment. What are the things you could do each day that would let you be more like the Fool? Write out how you restrict yourself from daring to trust the outcome. Do you spend your time worrying over things you can't control? If so, how can you let that go? What can you do daily to let your intuition lead you more than your worried mind? Once you've written your answers, begin to practice it.

Daring to Trust the Inner Voice

As Witches we are armed with intuition, and this inner voice is a vital weapon in our arsenal. Daring to listen to ourselves even if what we know to be true is contrary to the information presented to us, takes strength. Believing without a doubt in our gut instincts requires conviction and a confidence in our own power. Trusting this gift is a hard-won endeavor that takes time and effort to develop.

Intuition is something all humans possess. It often makes itself known through our clairsenses. The problem with listening to our intuition lies in our own deep-seated issues of self-doubt, blame, or judgment. These are problems that become embedded in us from childhood and they become our greatest hurdles in connecting to our intuition. We stop listening to our inner voice and instead doubt that we are correct. Sometimes we find ourselves unsure of whether or not our instinctive understanding of a situation is actually a judgment we ought not make. Other times we might feel as though we are just blame-shifting in order to come to terms with something. In actuality though, if we examine all the times our intuition gave us insight into a circumstance juxtaposed with how often we ignored that intuition, we'd recognize that we should have paid attention to what our intuition was trying to help us see.

Sometimes you might have a knowing that contradicts all the information you have on a subject. Whether it's your partner's fidelity or your job stability, all the facts say you can trust the integrity of the situation but you know something is up. To be daring is to listen to that knowing, question the validity of your comfort level with the assumed status quo, and ultimately seek the truth at all costs.

How many times have you had the idea that something was going to happen only to dismiss it because you didn't trust your own intuition? Perhaps while driving into work you think to yourself that you should take an alternate route. The detour would only add a minute or two of travel time. The thought comes to you more than once. As you approach the turn to make the detour, you decide against it. Maybe you feel guilty or get a sinking feeling but you continue forward on your course. Then, down the road a bit you come into a traffic jam that makes you late for work. What happened was your intuition communicated to you that the traffic jam was up ahead. It tried to warn you, but you second-guessed yourself and it led to a delay.

If you had dared to listen to yourself, you wouldn't be late for work. If you had let your intuition lead you, you may have had a much better day. Identifying when to listen to your inner voice isn't necessary—you should *always* do so. When you dare to, good things tend to happen. Your true inner voice is a message from the Source; the self-doubt, blame, and judgment are self-conscious responses to messages coming through. Learning to follow through with listening to your intuition will greatly increase the magick in your life. This is one reason why to Dare is so vital an aspect of magick.

Daring to trust the inner voice we hear can be unsettling, but that's only because we may not be used to listening to it. Developing as a Witch will help you learn to trust your intuition more and more as it proves itself to be correct. The key is to understand that your intuition will guide you and allow yourself to accept that guidance received from the Source at all times. To Dare is to surrender to the messages you can't fully understand. It allows you to find a closer connection to the Source through trust. In doing so your intuition becomes stronger. At the same time, we begin to understand ourselves better, allowing us to break through the fog of everyday life and better identify what it is we truly desire.

TRY THIS
What Does Your Inner Voice Say You Want?

In this practice, you will attempt to hear your inner voice and then learn to understand what it is trying to tell you.

What You'll Need
- Paper and a pen—If you like, you can use your journal for this exercise.

The Process

In a place where you won't be interrupted, sit for a moment and focus on your breathing. As you breathe in, feel your body relax. When you breathe out, let all your worries leave with your breath. Set the intention that you want to know your innermost thoughts. Decide that you want these thoughts to show up in a moment when you start writing.

With eyes closed, start moving your pen on the paper. Don't try to form letters or words, just let the pen glide across the paper freely. Keep thinking about your intention as you start to move the pen faster. Let your intuition lead your hand. Don't second-guess any movement you make—simply go with it. Do this until you feel like you are finished.

Once complete, open your eyes and see what you have written. Are there words? Have you drawn something? Is there anything discernible at all?

It is possible that nothing noticeable is on the page. That's okay if that's the case. Practicing this exercise consistently will eventually produce results. Do not feel defeated if it hasn't.

If you do see something on the paper, take note as to what it is. Did you know this was something you felt? What the mind produces when you aren't running the show can reveal a lot about how you really feel on a subject. From here, it is up to you to go deeper and learn all you can about what showed up on the paper.

Daring to Accomplish Your Dreams

Being a Witch in modern times has a lot to do with radical self-improvement. Whether we are seeking knowledge, power, status, or anything else, daring to better ourselves has become essential to Witchcraft. No matter where you are in life, there is always another level to be reached. From going into business for yourself, to learning, and even writing a first book, Witches these days are daring to chase down dreams more often than ever before.

Understanding that there is room for growth is the first step to developing a deeper understanding of what it will take to improve on our present circumstances. Daring to branch out and reach further is powerful. Recognition of the fact that there is more road to journey upon takes strength. When I was homeless in Summerville, I knew I had further to go. Seeking out direction was difficult. Not every opportunity that came along worked out for me, but that's the point of being daring. Trying everything that piqued my interest couldn't be the wrong choice when I had nothing to lose. For a lot of people, this can be an intimidating endeavor. The fear of failure is often present in these beginning stages. To be daring is to ask yourself what would you do if you knew you couldn't fail. And then once you are able to answer this question, the next logical choice is to go out and do it.

As Witches, when we strive to become more we are accessing the power of the pillar To Dare. We are setting our sights on a goal and then bravely moving forward in a new direction that ultimately allows us to live our best Witchy lives. This is an active attempt to manifest our desires. Daring to accomplish our dreams is magick because we are jumping into the unknown, listening to our inner voices, and honoring ourselves in the process. When we take action to see our desires come into fruition we are daring to love ourselves.

JOURNAL PROMPT
What Would You Do?

Write out exactly what you would want to do if you could not fail at anything. Make a list or focus on one thing. Once you know what you would set your intentions on if failure was not an issue, start listing all the things you would have to accomplish to see this dream come to fruition.

Now that you have a layout of what you want and how to accomplish it, start working on this goal.

Dare to Love Yourself

Self-care is important for all humans. Witches in particular tend to be much more aware of its importance. Loving yourself first is an act of daring that is sometimes mistaken as selfish. But this is not true because when we dare to love ourselves we are making a concerted effort to ensure that we are receiving the care that we need. Witches work with energies. It is imperative for us to recognize when negativity in our environment is affecting us. Doing the work to rid our lives of that negativity is an act of bravery. Too often the source of negativity that is oppressing us is linked to some other area of our lives. If we fail to take the time to remove a source of oppression or gloom it ultimately results in an inevitable undesirable effect on our magick.

Family can sometimes get in the way of our own self-care. We don't all get to choose where we live and who we are around. Often this is the case in the younger years of our lives when our autonomy is hindered by our inability to obtain true independence. It is common to feel stuck in situations that are out of our control. In this situation it is important to find ways to love yourself despite your environment. Being in situations that rob us of certain levels of independence does not mean we are powerless. Finding the time to focus on yourself is still very much an attainable thing.

Often we might find that a domestic partner interferes with our own care. This could be weighing down magickal expression. Remember that allowing that environment to persist is not always a choice, but all the same don't forget that you are a Witch though. You have power. There may be a tough choice to make in this circumstance but tough choices are part of being daring. Asserting yourself and taking action is the obvious first step. In the most optimal of situations, you'll get a good outcome. If working on change doesn't work, perhaps leaving the environment temporarily or even for good is the only option.

Daring to do what is right for your own self-care is never the wrong choice. There are times when practical safety measures must be set in place as part of getting out of negative relationships. It might be hard and uncomfortable at first but, the bravery it takes to let go of these situations is literally what makes the pillar to

Dare so magickal. You are empowered to bravely go into the world of the unknown and you have the ability to manipulate the positive energy of that choice to better yourself in the long run.

Daring to love yourself is the best aspect of this pillar. Literally taking the steps to say and show the world, "Hey, I come first for me," allows us to stand in our own power. We are essentially taking authority and governing ourselves. Even if things fall apart around you at first, the fact that you made a decision to love yourself instead of letting a bad situation hold you back only ends in positive outcomes. The important thing to do next is to let go of the pain or frustration the bad situation may have caused. Holding on to such things will only continue to get in your way.

TRY THIS
How Do You Love You?

Have a great time with this practice.

What You'll Need
- Nothing, you're the boss.

The Process
Take a moment to think about what you deserve. How do you prefer to pamper yourself? Do you like massages, manicures, fishing, or anything else? For one whole day, do only what you want to do for yourself. If you have responsibilities like children or chores, plan ahead: set up a block of time that you can use for just yourself and then go out and do what you want. This will revitalize you. If it feels like work, it is not self-care.

Shadow Work

There are deeper parts of ourselves that we tend to resist, one of which would be our shadow self. Acknowledging our shadow selves requires us to be daring. This is a side of us that is made up of all the things we have been told we shouldn't be, most often jealous, angry, and addicted.

What first creates this part of us is the response to our actions we receive from others. We learn from their reactions to us at a young age what is and isn't acceptable socially. This continues as we grow into adulthood. Over time we are taught that fits of rage are undesirable, self-doubt is weakness, and several other natural reactions or behaviors are looked down upon. We learn from those around us that these things could hinder or threaten our social acceptance. Because of this, we begin to hide those parts of us away. We do this so well that our shadow self becomes unrecognizable to us. We begin to believe these behaviors are not a part of our own personality.

It's common that we notice those very same shadow behaviors in other people only to be annoyed by them. We will often avoid those who remind us subconsciously of the parts of ourselves we are trying to hide away, a phenomenon called projection. When our shadow is out of control, it's easy for us to react to these people in negative and sometimes hostile ways. This is one reason learning to tame your shadow is essential to developing as a Witch.

To Dare is to know these parts of ourselves and to own them. To bravely confront our shadows gives us the upper hand. It allows us to understand our reactions to others as well as our motivations behind our visible behaviors. For instance, sometimes our shadow selves will push us in the opposite direction of our desired behavior. An example of this would be a person who avoids self-doubt to such an extent that they present themselves as overly confident to anyone paying attention. Learning to identify this part of ourselves helps us reel in an opposing behavior that might be just as obnoxious.

Even in my worst moments no one would know that I deal with depression on a near daily basis. This is because I present an overly optimistic person to the world. While I was homeless in Summerville, there was no indication that I was so depressed or that I wanted to die. In all honesty, I didn't realize it myself until things were really bad. And once things got better I went back to being unaware. It wasn't until many years later when I started to confront my shadow that I learned it was normal to feel the way I did. I came to understand that when I gave my depression space to exist, it didn't drag me so far down into suicidal ideation. As I learned to identify my shadow's needs, I was able to let it out of hiding from time to time. This allowed me to find peace with my depression. In turn I have been able to experience true happiness.

None of us are perfect and shadow work can be some of the scariest stuff we deal with as Witches. Regardless of what you recognize in yourself, working on those things is going to be hard. Daring to take the steps to heal yourself of codependency might bring up a lot of fear of loneliness just as identifying why you make inappropriate jokes in uncomfortable situations may lead you to actually dealing with your feelings.

No matter what, you're highly likely to face things you don't want to face if you're working on your shadow. Daring to work on these things helps you to better know yourself. In this way you are beginning to really learn about yourself, and knowing yourself is an important part of being a Witch.

JOURNAL PROMPT
What Bothers You About Others?

Write about a behavior that bothers you the most in someone else. Why does it bother you? Where did this disdain for that behavior come from? Did you learn to dislike this from something in your past?

JOURNAL PROMPT
What Feeling Would You Give Up?

What is one emotion you feel that you wish you didn't? Why don't you want to feel this way? What is the experience of feeling this way like for you?

JOURNAL PROMPT
Do You Like You?

What is something you don't like about yourself? Why do you feel that way? Who taught you to feel that way? How can you change the narrative about this feeling?

Suggested Reading

Initiated: Memoir of a Witch by Amanda Yates Garcia. Grand Central Publishing, 2019.

Waking the Witch: Reflections on Women, Magic, and Power by Pam Grossman. Gallery Books, 2019.

9
To Will

The most magickal tool a Witch has is their will. To Will is to manifest. A Witch's will is their discipline and conviction, the effort they are willing to put into seeing their magick come to fruition. Magickal intention is where our will resides, but it goes beyond that. The level of faith a Witch possesses is a testament to their will, as is the approach to mundane life.

Witchcraft is not all about cauldrons and athames; it has almost nothing to do with chalices, wands, or pentacles. You don't need an altar to be a Witch, and you are not more magickal just because you have every crystal known to humankind or fifteen decks of tarot cards. What makes anyone magickal is the intention placed behind their spells. Herbs and candles are not a necessity, they are just physical representations of our true magick—our will.

"Will" is a multi-faceted word that has a myriad of meanings, all of which have the same core definition: action. We will things into being or will ourselves not to eat all the cake; conversely, we will get the groceries out of the car or pay the bills. And action itself is power above anything else. Action is all the steps we take to make anything happen. When we decide to keep trying or to give up, we are taking action. When we light a candle, or look for a job, we are taking action. This is the act of will.

To Will is a pillar or Witchcraft because the will of a Witch is everything. It takes will to Be Silent and to Dare. And what good is what we know if we don't take action to put that knowledge to use? When a Witch casts a spell, they believe in what they are doing; their faith that the magick will work is the main ingredient of their spell. They decide that this thing they want will happen, that it will come to them. And then they go out and work hard to ensure that they see the reciprocity of their actions. To Will is to first believe in what we can accomplish and then go out and give it our all until we reach the finish line. That is magick, that is why to Will is a pillar. Without a will, magick can't be held up.

To Will starts in our mundane lives, from the effort we put into our education and jobs to the parts of ourselves we sacrifice for the greater good of a relationship. To be willing is necessary in order to navigate the world around us. We must be willing to overcome our obstacles, to see things through to the end. It is up to us to will ourselves through the work day or to do all that we must to survive a sickness. We will ourselves through our workouts, diets, and interactions with emotionally draining people. As a result, we receive our rewards, like promotions or fitness. Why, then, wouldn't this principle apply to magick?

Obstacles, roadblocks, and setbacks are familiar for pretty much anyone; at some point, things will not the way we want. It's like a rite of passage to jump through hoops or over hurdles in order to obtain what we desire. How we deal with these moments is what defines us as people. It speaks of how willing we are to endure in order to gain what we desire. To Will is to acknowledge that nothing less than our expectations will be accepted.

My Story: Will In Action

I never wanted to drop out of high school; it was my goal even in my early teen years to go to college. My ideas of what I would study changed fluidly as I grew up but higher education was always an intention for me. Being a homeless teen and young adult ruined that dream for nearly a decade, but once the Witches took me in, my dreams began to flower again. Between sleeping on their couch to having my own room in a friend's house, college began to seem more attainable. Transportation was an issue but for the first time in a long while I knew that I could see the opportunity approach on the horizon. I took a summer to work in a traveling carnival in a head shop. We sold incense, rock and roll tapestries, and glass pipes. When I came back, I became determined to find my way into school.

First, I needed someone to show me how to not live in poverty. Living in my friend's trailer with plastic in place of glass in the window wasn't going to cut it. I sought out older men who were looking for a young guy to care for. Morally I knew it was inappropriate but at the time I lacked morals and so I stopped at nothing to prey on these men who likely saw me as the hunted. Eventually I found a guy who owned a porn website. In exchange for my company and some work in his office, he offered me a place to live.

In a short period of time, I started talking about wanting to go to school. He had developed feelings for me, and, while it might not have been ethical, I faked the reciprocity of those feelings. He was addicted to meth and cocaine; I wanted to climb out of poverty. I did all the grocery shopping for this man and he paid the bills. I cleaned our house and he let me use the car as often as I wanted. When I enrolled in community college, he was happy for me at first, although it wasn't long before he saw where things were heading. I started saving all my loan refund checks and found myself a part-time job. He started bringing new guys home and attempted to lure me into group sessions. I declined and it created tension.

As I made new friends at school, I found people who lived near the campus. Instead of using the guy's car, I started getting rides to class. As my third semester started, I found a new place to live, a one-bedroom apartment that three of us rented. When I moved out of the older guy's house, he thought I was leaving for school for the day, but really I had been slowly moving my clothes out for a week. Once free of the drug addict, I began looking into four-year schools and willing a person into my life who would help me become a more functioning adult.

I wanted to study art and I wanted to begin creating in the place where I was created, so I found an art school in Philadelphia. I applied and was accepted. It can be a scary thing to move to a city you know nothing about. It can be scarier not knowing anyone there, but I knew I would make friends. It was easy because I lived in the dorms. The only problem was that everyone was younger than me. Within a week, I found the local gay bars and began to frequent them. It was in doing this that I met one of the best friends I have had in my life.

Mark was not a Witch, at least as far as I know, but it was through him that I learned how to live with intention. Before we met, I was meandering through life unsure of what I wanted or how to get it. But Mark showed me that once I knew what I was after, I needed to work for it. I needed to ensure that all my actions led to the outcome I desired. Mark raised me, and taught me that I was worth being loved and how to love myself. I was a twenty-five-year-old child when we met. Through his tutelage, I was a twenty-eight-year-old man when I graduated college.

If I Had Known

I went from attempting to strangle myself under a bridge to having a bachelor's degree. It took me eight years to see this development come about. From the moment I dared to keep going, I began to will a change into existence. I needed help first and it came to me naturally. In order to become the Witch I am today, I was going to need a new environment, new people to show me the way. If I had known all along that I could have willed these things into my life it might not have taken me as long to reach my end game. The journey, though, is what made it worth it.

Meeting a drug-addicted sugar daddy and using him as a stepping stone was an essential part of my path, though I can look back now and see why I should not have behaved that way. I now understand the reason taking advantage of anyone is wrong. At the time, I thought I was willing my way forward but in truth what I was doing was ethically inappropriate. What I know now about magick is that taking advantage of a person is not enacting my will but rather an act of deceit. In that moment of my life, I was being willful to ensure my survival but not in a way required by magick. If I had known how to use my will correctly, I might have avoided causing someone else pain.

I thought I was finding someone to show me the way but really he was just a cog in the machine of my will at work. His assistance led to college and college led to Mark. I didn't really find my way until I met Mark, until the interaction was mutual and no one was being taken advantage of. I willed him into my life because I needed someone to love me, someone who could help me grow, and someone who would selflessly teach me to love myself and others without the expectation of romantic or sexual contact of any sort.

What I didn't understand about will was its power to help me manifest what I needed. Even after I made it through college I figured I could will things into my life instantly. And though there are people who can do this, that was not the case for me at the time. I didn't understand all the aspects of will. Because will encompasses so many things even in the Witching world, it is necessary for a practitioner to understand all the nuances of this pillar to really access the power of will.

To Will is to have conviction in one's belief system. This means that it is imperative to believe without a doubt that what we are manifesting will come to us. The act of will falters when we find ourselves unsure of whether or not we can accomplish our goals. I believed in myself and my ability to go further. Often during my trials I was not sure of myself, but I pushed that uncertainty away. I stuffed it down and refused to believe in anything other than the idea that I could achieve my goals. In the end I received exactly what I wanted because I had a system of belief. I believed in me.

Discipline is also imperative in regard to will as it takes commitment in order to exert this power into the world. If we fail to be steadfast in our will then we are likely to lose our motivation. This results in spells that fall short of our desired outcome.

How one applies their magical skills is an act of will. No one is on the same magickal path as anyone else. My journey is vastly different from that of my sister's and all of my Witchy friends. Because of this, how I choose to make my magick manifest is going to be different as well. I work with the sun and the moon, with candles and herbs, and with a specific deity. Because those things resonate for me, my will is easily accessed in order to see the fruits of my labor.

Finally, the approach a person takes in both their mundane and magickal life informs the will they put into the world. A person who is determined to see things through and not give up is willing their success in every action they take. When I decided I would find someone to teach me how to be an adult on my terms, I sought it out. When I wanted to get into college, I actively pursued it until I got what I wanted.

Willing the Magick

A fire can start with a single spark and a little accelerant; if it is allowed to burn uncontrolled, it can quickly become a battle wrought with casualties and devastation. It is no wonder that to Will is associated with the element of fire. From its use in rituals to cooking, or from forging metal to creating heat and light, fire is almost literally an act of will. It can destroy or sustain life based solely on intention. A fire that is out of control can be like a war, when you think about it a willful person is not much different.

When using magick, Witches are accessing the ability to burn through any opposition that stands in their way. While an act of will in the realm of magick is often used to deal with an obstacle, the process to do so is quite different than it is when one is using daring to overcome. With will, one does not overcome their obstacles but rather burns through them. In relation to daring, overcoming an obstacle means going around or finding another path. Where will is concerned, the practitioner is more intent on removing the obstacle rather than taking a detour.

Just as with fire, will must be handled with care otherwise it can create damage and destruction in the wake of its path. The use of will in magick requires its practitioner to remain steadfast and clear on their intention. Like a glass containing wax from a candle, we must also protect others from our will. This is why to Will is a pillar of Witchcraft—will can both nourish and destroy.

In magick when we set our intentions, we create the spark. Our will is also the accelerant. How much will or effort we put into seeing our outcomes come to fruition determines whether we produce a raging forest fire or a cozy campfire to keep us warm on an autumn night.

Willing the spells that we cast to become fulfilled intentions is predicated on the mundane work we put behind our magick. If we don't keep the fires stoked, we lose steam and the engine slows down. Conversely, we risk losing control altogether if the fire burns too bright. The magick of will comes in discerning exactly when to use it and how much is necessary for our outcomes. Because our intentions are so intricately connected to our will, magick doesn't really work without it. Just as the combustion in an engine moves a vehicle forward, the ability to will does the same for magick.

JOURNAL PROMPT
Set Your Will to Your Intentions

Write out an intention you want to work on. Without worrying about the outcome, take time to map out all the actions you will take to see the intention come to pass. What behaviors are necessary to get what you want? If you were not using magick at all, how would you get your intention to become a reality?

The Will of Liquid Fire

There is a myth about a goddess named Pele where she takes a canoe from Tahiti and ends up at the Hawaiian Islands. When she reached the islands, she began to try to set her fires but has been pursued by her sister, who wants to kill her. Pele migrates throughout the islands only to be eventually overtaken and destroyed by her sister … but the story didn't end there. Even though Pele was physically destroyed she continued on, unencumbered by the loss of her flesh. She grew to become known as the goddess of volcanoes and fire. To this day she is still honored with hula dances despite the Christianization and colonization of Hawaii. Even tourists fear her—those who steal pieces of the volcanic land return it once they have had their fill of bad luck brought on by Pele's curse.

When I think of deities and the magick of will, Pele is the one who comes to mind first. Her fierceness is evident in the idea that she resides in the heart of a volcano. Coupled with the fact that she is so well known of all Polynesian deities even today speaks volumes. Considering Pele's connection to volcanoes and therefore lava, it's easy to see how this goddess can be worked with in terms of will.

When a volcano erupts, the lava it spews forth is a force none can reckon with. Lava engulfs all things; the only recourse is to get out of its way. It is this idea that can be invoked when working with Pele. The power of the Goddess and the determination of lava can be imbued into your intentions and thus empower your magick.

TRY THIS
Pele Power Up

This spell will call upon the deity to make your will like lava. You will be petitioning Pele to infuse your magick with a little extra strength from her fiery presence.

What You'll Need
- Red candles, three total
- A bowl of water
- A volcanic stone (Hint: you can find this type of rock in most hardware stores in the outdoor grill section. Obsidian works well for this also.)
- An orange cut into equal sections

The Process

Carve your intention and the name of Pele into each of the red candles. Set the candles in a triangle around your bowl of water and place your volcanic rock in the water. Call your intention out loud say all the mundane things you can do to bring this intention about. Once finished, light the first candle while asking Pele to help you. Repeat these steps for each candle.

Once the three candles are lit, ask Pele to make your will like lava. Repeat again your intention and the actions you will take to see the intention through. Then request that she allow your actions to move like lava through any obstacles that may stand between you and your goals. Once finished, sit in meditation until your candles burn out. During this time, focus on the actions you have said you will take and visualize yourself in lava form taking those steps to reach your goal.

When the candles burn out, clean up your candles and the bowl with the rock and water. Leave in their place the sliced orange as an offering to the goddess.

The Will You Use Is the Same

When we want something in our mundane lives, we set our goal, work to achieve our desired outcome, and then gain our reward in the end. Of course, all of this requires a carefully laid out plan. The magickal process works in this same way, too. On the surface, our approach to achieve our goals might appear very different from a magickal point of view as opposed to a mundane one. The truth is that they are not different at all. For any endeavor, we must first set our sights on the goal. Next we must put in the work to obtain the desired outcome. And finally, we are rewarded once we achieve our goal. In very basic terms, getting what we want requires the same thing—will. Regardless of whether it is a mundane or magickal undertaking, the will we use is the same.

With magick, the difference is at the point where we must believe in a more abstract process. For mundane goals, we know that if we want to gain a healthier, fit body it requires a proper diet and exercise routine. There's a lot of science and information that informs this knowledge, so it is easy to accept and follow through. In magick, there isn't a specific tried and true method to pull off anything. Magick is so diverse, and it comes from so many different cultures. There are a plethora of ways to work on the same outcome. The hurdles we meet with in magick are not whether or not we can exert our will on the desire, but rather in ascertaining whether we are using the method that is right for us to do so.

Putting the work into seeing our desires come to fruition is not the hard part of magick. We are already doing this sort of thing in our mundane lives. We already know that hard work pays off. Willing anything into our mundane world is identical to willing something in our magickal one. The difference is that for mundane matters, we have solid processes that everyone uses, (such as working to make money), whereas our magickal process is based on the individual practitioner. Knowing that the choices I made for a road opener spell were the right ones for me can be the hardest aspect of magick. Because there are so many options and paths that we could choose from, identifying the right one for ourselves becomes an issue that could provide us with more doubt than comfort.

The manner in which an individual applies magick to their lives is complex. It should never be doubted. When it comes to magick, there isn't a single approach that will always work for everyone. We live in a world that is inundated with so much information and so many ideas on how something should be done. Learning to sort through all of that information to find your own path is an act of will because only you can take the metaphoric machete in hand and cut down the overgrowth to your liking.

JOURNAL PROMPT
What Works for You

Write down all the times magick has worked in your favor. Do a personal inventory of every spell you have ever cast. Then ask yourself, did I get what I wanted? If the answer is yes, make a list of all the things you did to ensure the outcome. Was it a specific kind of magick? Did it revolve around a certain kind of intention? Whatever you can think of that helped your magick along matters here.

Align Your Will

In regard to Will in magick, it is important to remember that this is an issue of what we believe and how we apply will to that belief. If you believe that your magick only works within specific restrictions, then that is exactly how it will pan out. In other words, what works for my sister will not always work for me. While some principles of magick are the same for all practitioners, not all processes will work for all people.

I love fire. Since I was a child, I have always been mesmerized by this element. As I have grown up, I have learned that there is a great reason for this. At first I thought it was because I am an Aries, but as I dove deeper into understanding myself, I learned that my natal chart is packed full of fire signs. In fact, the only other element in my chart is air. I have an affinity of fire because that is what I am primarily made up of. When I apply my magickal skills, I always use fire because I know that for me, it is the best way to place my will into my magick.

Now when I craft spells I make sure that there are always candles and often a fire pit involved. I send my spells up in smoke or bury them in places where I will then build fires. This is how I am able to align my will to work with my magick.

My sister is not a fire sign; in fact when there is only one fire sign in her whole chart. Therefore, her magick would not work under the same circumstances as mine. Fire does not resonate with her. I could share with her all the info I have on why doing things my way works well but, those practices would not align with her will because she is not a fire sign.

Accessing our will is not the easiest feat, or at least not at first. We require conviction in order to put our will into anything. If I did not like going to the gym or only wanted to eat sugary and fried foods, I become fit even if I went through the motions to do so. I would fail at some point and go right back into the habits that led me to an unfit lifestyle. The same holds true for magick.

If my deity leads me to use modern names to work with them but I am taking classes that insist on using old Greek names, I am not going to gain as much from the lessons. I could try to put all my will into the classes. I could do my best to find them enthralling and helpful, but at some point my discipline for the class would fade—what I'm doing doesn't resonate with what I want to put my will into.

TRY THIS
The Will to Fail

We all know our strengths, but what about our weaknesses? For this exercise seek out a spell that does not resonate with you. If you normally work with one element, find a spell that requires a different one. Take the path you don't travel. Start small with a ritual that has little consequence. Explore a side of your magick you shy away from using, but don't dive into the deep end. Search the internet for a spell that fits an intention you might have but goes against the grain of your own personal magick. Maybe it is a jar spell or a meditation. Whatever *doesn't* suit you is the goal here. Take the time to see and experience the magick that doesn't work in your favor. Be sure that whatever intention you are setting isn't a make-or-break kind of situation. This exercise is meant to make you a little uncomfortable, not throw you out of whack or ruin your life.

To Will Takes Discipline

The will expressed in discipline is likely the easiest to identify. This is because when we look at a person we can see the evident results of their discipline. Success takes discipline. It isn't hard to see a person who works out every day and point out how successful they are at it based on how well-built their body is. The same can be said about an artist who paints in their free time; we are able to see the evidence of their discipline in the artwork they are producing. There are two caveats to discipline in relation to magick: the evidence of our discipline is not likely to be tangible, and there is no true gauge for the discipline of a Witch.

Let's be clear right away, it is no one's business how disciplined any Witch is compared to another. That said, a Witch's discipline may not be as readily evident as the discipline of a weightlifter. While the Witch and the gym rat experience results from their discipline; a person who works out has visible results whereas the Witch's results are often not immediately evident to everyone.

When a Witch is disciplined, they could be doing all sorts of things in a daily practice that no one will ever see. Meditation, gratitude, divination, and deity dedication are just a few things that Witches do each day that no one witnesses. Considering that the first pillar of Witchcraft is to Keep Silent, it is no surprise that discipline for a Witch often is not readily apparent. While our daily practices are our discipline, it is not something even we, as individuals, might be able to quantify. After a while, a Witch might not realize just how much discipline they are placing into their magick. It is important for this reason that we consistently check in with ourselves. We don't want to go overboard and neglect other parts of our lives any more than we want to slack and lose our connection to the Source.

JOURNAL PROMPT
Daily Practice Inventory

What are your daily practices? Do you believe you are able to keep up your practice without incident? If not, how can you adapt your practice to better fit into your life and maintain your discipline?

Magick Will Work

The power of our will resides in that which each Witch believes to be true. By definition, if we do not believe our magick will work, it simply won't. To Will is to force our belief into the actions we take. When we experience self-doubt, we impede our magick and potentially counteract it.

When a Witch casts a spell, they are placing intentions out into the world. These intentions are put in things like candles and poppets and several other things that serve as a physical representation of our will. If we fail to believe in the magick that has been placed in those things, our magick is likely to fall short. This is because our will is not tested.

For example, if I want to find money to pay a bill and start second-guessing my process, I am actually second-guessing myself. I would be literally putting my own conviction into question. Whether I consciously or subconsciously do this doesn't matter because at the end of the day, what I have done is failed to believe in the power of my own will.

When we question our own conviction, we are not placing will into our magick as much as we are placing will into our doubt. If we fail to be sure of ourselves, we not only lose the magickal connection we share with the Source but also the connection we have invested into seeing our desires come to fruition. If we sever these connections, we are left unable to will our endeavors into being.

What we believe and how we believe it is never up for question by anyone else. If we find ourselves questioning these things, we must take the time to identify why. As well, we must do all we can to try and push these feelings away from our minds. Using the skills of discipline is one way to come up against these feelings of self-doubt.

JOURNAL PROMPT
What Causes You Doubt?

Think back on all the times you have worked your magick. In those times what created the most doubt in you? How did that doubt affect your will to keep working to see your goal come into being? How could you combat that doubt in the future?

Willpower and the Mundane

I would be remiss if I did not include the subject of willpower, the determination that allows someone to do something difficult. When a person wants to quit smoking, they have to be determined to do so; otherwise, they will be tempted by the vice and potentially fail. In terms of magick, the idea of willpower plays out in the mundane world.

If an intention for a spell is set to gain financial independence but then the Witch who cast the spell isn't saving money, it's not likely they will find the independence they are seeking. When working magick and considering the mundane action necessary for that magick to work, it is imperative that one exercises willpower as one of those mundane actions. Failing to exhibit self-control is a path to failed magick, especially when that magick requires one to show a little restraint in order to see results.

Anyone can say they want something but if actions don't line up with wants, disappointment is likely to follow. Mundane actions are important because that is the real work when it comes to magick. What we do after the spell matters as much, if not more than the spell we cast. If you want a job, you have to search for one. In that same vein, if you want to save money, you'd better be saving it every chance you get. This means using restraint and discipline as the mundane work after the magick work is complete.

TRY THIS
The Stop Candle

This is a candle spell to help you build up your willpower and stop yourself when temptation presents itself.

What You'll Need
- A red seven-day candle

The Process
Every morning when you wake up, think about the current goal you are working on: a diet, a plan to save money, or any other mundane thing that requires willpower. Light your red seven-day

candle and look into the flame. Think about the things that could tempt you to falter in your goal. While staring at the flame, consider your feelings if you did not reach the goal you set for yourself. Then focus on the candle's red color and say, "Not today." Then blow it out. As you do this, visualize yourself blowing all the temptations out with the flame. If you find yourself tempted throughout your day to do what you ought not to, picture the candle and say out loud, "Stop, not today." Then blow as if you are blowing out the flame and the temptations once again.

You Will, Don't Worry

To Will is to use the power within you to get what you want. This manifests in several ways. You might will yourself to resist temptation or exert your will over a situation. You could power through an obstacle in your way, or ensure that your magick and your will align. Whether you are using magick or not, you are using the power of will every day.

This pillar exists regardless of what structure it is holding up. Considering this, it shouldn't be a hard transition into our magickal life. After all, we use our will on a daily basis. Once we become aware that we are tapping into this ability though we become more powerful. It is in knowing that we are using will that Witches gain strength. The foundation of this pillar is already set. When a Witch accesses this pillar they are just creating a focal point in an already profoundly strong and complex structure. The beauty of the building housing magick for all its practitioners is that even when one pillar is more obvious than the others they are all still working equally.

To Will is likely the most in-your-face pillar of Witchcraft because, like a fire, you just can't miss it. It is hard not to see when one's will is at work in their magick. After all an intention is literally what a Witch is willing into existence.

Suggested Reading

Instant Magick: Ancient Wisdom, Modern Spellcraft by Christopher Penczak. Llewellyn Publications, 2006.

10
To Know

Witchcraft is often called "the path of the wise" for a reason: as Witches, we are constantly on a journey of learning. If we are lucky, we grow to understand ourselves and the universe around us over time. We gain insight about spiritual practices. As we develop, we learn to harness the energy of the sun, moon, celestial events, the seasons, and our own emotions. We become one with our shadow and come to terms with the idea that we are imperfect. Being a Witch has less to do with the spells we cast than it does with the way we chose to interact with the world around us, both the seen and the unseen. Understanding our motivation helps us discern our true needs, it helps us identify our honest desires. Knowing ourselves is, above all other things, one of the most important jobs a Witch has.

To Know is the final pillar of Witchcraft. Knowing informs the other three pillars because it allows a Witch to understand the purpose behind their will, daring, and silence. To Know holds up the structure of magick because without knowledge there is no connectedness. Why would you dare to do something if you don't know why it would be daring? How could you will something into existence if you don't understand the intricacies of how will works? Finally, what good is your silence if the reason for it is not clear? Beyond informing the other pillars, the power of knowledge also stands on its own.

Witchcraft is a collection of wisdom that has been passed down over thousands of years. From the *Greek Magical Papyri* and the *Chaldean Oracles* to books by Silver RavenWolf, Scott Cuningham, and Judika Illes, there are innumerable resources from which to glean information. Education is what helps a Witch create a practice that is both powerful and effective. We are always evolving, even when we don't realize it. When we seek out more knowledge we allow ourselves to develop organically, maintaining a constant state of change.

Through seeking knowledge of the world around us, we learn to better harness the energies of plants, elements, and timing. Knowing how our magick works informs our spells and rituals. Understanding why we would use a mustard seed or the full moon helps us better manifest our goals. Understanding the resonance in the materials and processes we use in our workings allows us to connect on both an emotional and logical level to our correspondences. This is what gives our magick its strength.

Knowing our true desires allows us to cut through the shrubbery that would cloud our intentions. Instead of just wanting a new job, when we know ourselves we know that we want a job which frees us from the restrictions that leave us feeling marginalized or unfulfilled. When we are in touch with ourselves, we have a better understanding of what we really want out of our magick. Being aware in this way helps us to best focus our magick in order to manifest our goals.

To Know sets us up to be wise Witches for much more than the obvious reasons. Wisdom is about more than how much we know about a specific thing. To be wise is to know that you'll never know everything but you'll continue to seek out information regardless. It means you are aware that change is both constant and necessary in order to develop as a human and a Witch. And it means you understand why you do the magickal things that you do.

When we are actively pursuing knowledge we are growing our magick. As we become more aware of ourselves we understand how magick works through us. When we study the wisdom of the Witches who came before us, we learn new ways to access that magick. And as we grow to understand why correspondences work for specific reasons, we develop a deeper connection to the forces that fuel the manifestation of our desires. We become forces of nature in our own right as we learn and retain the knowledge we seek.

My Story: I Felt a Sense of Knowing

In 2008, five days after I turned twenty-seven, my right testicle was swollen three times its normal size. When I ejaculated, it looked as though I had sneezed dark green mucus into my hand. Needless to say, I was alarmed. I didn't have health insurance at the time, but I did know a doctor who was paying me for sex. He would see me after hours in his office and provided free medical care for me as needed. He ran all the STI tests on me. While we waited for the HIV test to show a result, all the other tests showed up negative. "It is probably an odd infection," he told me, then left the room to see about the HIV test.

When he walked back in he seemed somber. I said, "Well?"

He looked at me and sort of shrugged while saying, "It's not negative."

The world caved in around me. I couldn't see anything, I couldn't feel anything. I needed a cigarette. The doctor and I went around the back of his clinic to smoke. He asked me if I was okay, but I didn't answer. Although I wasn't shocked by the test results, I was alright. I had lived my life precariously up to that moment. It was no surprise to me that I would end up with HIV at some point. I had been prostituting since I was eighteen and not making the best choices while doing so. I was more shocked that all the other HIV tests I had been given over the last nine years *didn't* turn out positive. I was aware that at that point in time, HIV was not a death sentence. What really had me shaken up was that even though my symptoms had nothing to do with HIV, I knew that day would be the day I tested positive.

A couple months later, I started developing lumps all over my body. They were in my neck, underarm, and groin. On top of the lumps I started getting debilitating migraines that were so painful they caused me to vomit. Because of my HIV status, I finally had access to health care so I went to the doctor. They decided it was my immune system coming back online now that the HIV was controlled with medication; basically, it was trying to fight off everything it couldn't while the HIV ravaged my body. I was given a steroid and sent on my way. But two weeks later, the lumps had worsened and I was getting sicker.

I was watching a show one night where the main character was describing their lymphoma and it all came to me at once. I shot up from my bed and knew that what I was experiencing was related to my lymphatic system and there was cancer in it. I went back to the doctor and told them what I thought was going on. They sent me for a biopsy. When I called for the results, the doctor who gave them to me seemed sad. He confirmed that I did, in fact, have cancer and then he told me he was sorry. I spent more of that phone call consoling the doctor than I did getting my results. I knew I was going to be okay. I knew everything was going to be fine.

I went to school every day and worked hard to finish college. Over that year, I went from having some odd infection to testing positive. Then I walked around for months with lumps growing all over me only to learn they were caused by a type of cancer HIV patients normally get on their skin. I would leave class and walk across Center City Philadelphia to go get a chemo treatment only to head back to school so I could take another class or work on my graduate project. Eventually the cancer was tamed. I continued taking my HIV meds and the chemo sorted out the rest. Never once did I stop moving forward. Not one time did I think I would die from what was happening. In May 2009, I graduated from college with a 3.8 GPA. I knew I could make it, and I did.

If I Had Known

At the time, I had not even heard of claircognizance, yet that is what I experienced. When I look back over my life, I can see clearly all the moments that my sense of knowing informed what was about to happen. From the minor things to the big stuff, I had always had a knowing. If I had known that this was my magickal gift, I might have strengthened it. Instead, I went through life not knowing why I randomly knew stuff. Unfortunately, I also had no idea that I could have put it to use.

To Know is not directly related to this gift. Just because I know things for no reason doesn't mean I am tapping into this pillar of Witchcraft. We all possess a magickal gift; some have more than one. It is in knowing our gifts where the pillar of to Know comes into play.

Divine wisdom was handed to me through the Source for decades, and I did not know it was happening. For this reason, to Know is a pillar of Witchcraft: if I had known what was happening, I could have honed in on it and used it to my benefit. If I knew to listen to my magickal sense, I would have likely kept myself out of a lot of trouble in my younger years. Had I known how to strengthen this gift much sooner, I could have saved myself from several unfortunate events. It is only through seeking knowledge that I was able to grow my gift to what it is now. Today I know when the Source is speaking to me. And because I know, I stop to listen.

Knowing the Magick

The air around us is not visible. We can't see the wind, only the evidence of it in the rustling of leaves. Knowledge is like this as well which is why it makes sense that magickal practitioners associate it with the element of air. We can feel the wind on our skin at some times, and at others, it hides from us. Even then, we know it is there and that it exists. We have no idea what others know or don't know. Yet sometimes, a person's wisdom becomes evident in how they speak or what they choose to talk about. To Know is like air because it can go unnoticed and be ever-present.

To Know is to perform magick in a manner like the air. Air's power can be underestimated until it picks up like a tornado, leaving wreckage in its path. When using Witchcraft, what we know informs our power like the wind in a boat's sails. It can speed us along if there is enough of it but it can leave us stranded when it goes away.

The most amazing thing about knowing anything is that it can feed all the other information you have. Spells are strengthened in our understanding of *all* things, not just spell craft. What we know about science or language helps us to understand our magick too. Like the air around us, it can help a balloon lift off of the ground when heated by fire.

As an element, air is unique in that it interacts with the others in both constructive and destructive ways. It feeds a fire but can also extinguish one. Air assists in the movement of water as easily as it can cause it to evaporate. Wind can cause erosion and destruction throughout the earth but it is also a key factor in the propagation of plant life. In terms of magick, whatever we know can do this too. It isn't hard to reason with ourselves and find logical explanations to dismiss magickal happenings. As humans, we often want to explain things or understand how they work. This can create a disturbance when we cast spells that may leave us doubting because we think we "know better." But what we know about magick informs our spells and makes them powerful too.

To Know is to be steady like the air, to have an even understanding of magick and the world around us. It is to Know when we need the power of a gale force wind, or the calm of a still day. To Know is to always carry the secrets of our knowledge in our back pocket, to find comfort in knowing that if we need it, we could both stoke the fire or put it out. To Know is to rest assured that we can replenish the earth or erode away what doesn't serve us. And to Know is to be confident that we could create waves on the shore or eradicate all evidence that water ever touches a surface.

TRY THIS
Meditation with the Wind

On a windy day or before a storm, go outside with your journal and sit in silence. Let the wind blow all over you and close your eyes. Visualize the wisdom of the world floating in the wind itself. Clear your mind of all your personal thoughts. As the wind blows in your ears, listen for the information it whispers to you. Reach out with your magickal senses and see what comes to you. As you meditate, write down any messages or sensations you receive. Allow your mind to wander so that the wind itself can deliver you a message.

Sacrifices to Gain Knowledge

If we took the time to look at any pantheon, ancient or modern, we would find several gods and goddesses who are considered deities of knowledge or wisdom. Of all the deities I've ever learned about, none stand out in regard to knowledge as much as Odin. This Norse god was the Allfather not only because he was the parent to many gods of his pantheon but also because he was wise and shared that wisdom the way fathers do with their children. This deity above all others sought out knowledge with a fierceness that only a god could endure.

Wisdom is not easily obtained, and Odin made plenty of sacrifices to gain the knowledge. To learn of the runes, he bled and starved himself while hanging from Yggdrasil for nine days. Then, with his knowledge, he was able to create magick beyond any his contemporaries had seen. Odin was not only constantly seeking to know but often depicted as willing to teach. The amazing thing about Odin and his pursuit of knowledge is that he never believed he knew enough. He sought out information, often to his own detriment. It was he who pulled his eye from its socket in order to gain even more wisdom. If that's not a testament to the value of knowledge, I don't know what is.

Just like Odin sacrificed his eye for wisdom, it is likely a Witch will make a sacrifice for the knowledge they obtain as well. While it is unlikely we would be required to give our eye or any other body part in order to learn, we do sacrifice things like time and sometimes patience when we learn. In my case, my life of trauma led me to come out the other end a Witch who understands the necessity of pain for growth. We all make sacrifices for our wisdom. Sometimes the lessons we learn in life break us apart just so we can rebuild ourselves stronger than we were before. But in the end we *are* more powerful, armed with knowledge not only of who we are but also of what we can endure.

TRY THIS
Sacrifice Your Day

Do this practice on a Wednesday, Odin's day. You will have to plan ahead for this practice because it requires you to give up all things in your life for one day. You will need to take the day off from work, family, and your electronic devices. This practice also calls for a fast, but make sure that you are medically sound to do so. Do not put yourself in danger, and adapt if necessary. Instead of giving up everything, you can sacrifice only one thing and cast the spell accordingly.

What You'll Need
- A blue candle, the color of wisdom and knowledge, plus a tool for carving into the wax
- Your journal, to write the wisdom that comes to you

The Process

On a Wednesday, give up everything for one day from the time you wake up to the time you go to bed. Put your phone where you can't get it, don't work, don't read, don't eat, and drink only water for the day.

Light a blue candle and carve Odin's name into it. You can also carve the words "wisdom" and "knowledge" into the candle. Call out to Odin. Word your intention in your own way, but make sure to mention that since this is his day, you sacrifice your daily life as he did in order to gain magickal knowledge.

Spend the day alone. You should have no interactions if possible. While you are alone for the day, you can keep your journal with you. Spend the day contemplating magick and how to obtain more knowledge in your daily practice. When ideas and thoughts come to you, write them down. You can refer to your writing later as needed.

Pursuit of Knowledge

The knowledge we find on our journeys can come from a diverse number of places. That is exactly how we *should* learn our magickal practices, through multiple resources and various lessons. As we walk our path, we should always be on a mission to increase our education regardless of how much we think we know. Taking the time to fully learn from any outlet possible doesn't mean you're flaky or waffling. It means you are being a Witch. To truly know magick, to be a Witch, is to dive into information about more than just Witchcraft. Understanding psychology and other sciences help inform our magick. Taking the time to understand all paths of magick creates a cauldron of information we are able to dip into and fashion our own practices out of. Why not learn all you can about each path?

As Witches, we should be constantly learning. What you know and how much of it you assimilate is really what defines your magick. We all have different tastes, but if you find something interesting, take the time to dive deeper. That's how this whole learning thing works. It opens up areas of the world you didn't know existed. No writer has all the information. Taking the time to read works by people from other walks of life is helpful to really get to know yourself.

Magick is about evolving over time. We, as humans, don't evolve if we aren't learning. Sometimes that means we have to make sacrifices too.

JOURNAL PROMPT
Seek Information on Magickal Things You Don't Know

Begin researching herbs, deities, crystals, candle colors, magickal timing, or anything else you don't know about. This should be something that you aren't well versed in. If you know a lot about crystals do not waste this practice on that. If you chose to research deities be sure they are a part of a pantheon that you are uneducated in. This journal prompt should provide you with new information that will enhance your practice. You can come back to this entry over time and dive deeper into this new knowledge.

Who You Know Yourself to Be

To Know goes deeper than the information we seek in regard to Witchcraft. Knowing who we are as both people and Witches informs a lot of what we do in our spell crafting. Being aware of our moral limits, shadow self influence, and motivations helps to integrate all the parts of us into our magick. Many who start on the path of the wise are often led by some desire they are desperate to obtain. Typically this desperation is not their truth. It isn't who they really are. Desperation is normally fueled by the need to live up to some standard that should never have been imposed upon us. When we find ourselves deep in this way of thinking, it is likely that we have strayed from our true path. Only through careful self-reflection are we able to realign and become who we know ourselves to truly be.

No matter what the motivation that leads us to becoming a Witch, what matters is where we take our magick as we move farther down our path. There are Witches who spend all their lives in the pursuit of their initial endeavor. And while that is fine, it is often the case that Witches who try to understand their motivations tend to start approaching magick from new points of view with clearer goals.

Witchcraft is about improving our lives through magick.

All the money in the world won't solve issues related to self-acceptance. In fact, more money in our bank accounts would likely cause most of us to feel more stressed out by life in various new ways. We are told by society that we need money to feel safe, but that isn't true. What we need is stability and consistency.

The same holds true for most things. When it comes to love spells, we aren't really after the affections of specific people who fail to reciprocate our love. What we are really seeking is acceptance, loyalty, and companionship. Because we are affected by our past, we feel a need to work harder to earn something that should instead be given with minimal effort when we come up against opposition in the affairs of the heart.

When we know ourselves, it is easy to see that what we are seeking isn't a windfall or a lover who will love us back. What we need out of those situations is actually comfort. Once we are able to clearly identify our true intention, that intention is much easier to manifest. This is why knowing is magick.

It is through well-thought-out intentions that we can use our magick in order to manifest our true desires into our lives. Cutting through the surface issues to see what honestly lies beneath helps us to zero in on our true goal. It is only after we have done this work on ourselves that we will be able to cast the spells that will work for our own betterment.

JOURNAL PROMPT
Hone In on the Intention

Write out what you want: it might be money, love, fame, or anything else. Next dive deeper into understanding why this intention is your driving force. What does this want really boil down to? List the things that money, love, fame or anything else will bring for you. That list contains what it is you're really after. Next, choose just one aspect of the list you made. Could it be boiled down to more basic aspects? If so list those out. Do this until you find one single simple intention. Work on just that intention until you have it. Then go back to your list and repeat the process until you start to accumulate the basic desires.

Having a Firm Understanding

Once we know what we are really after, we need to know what corresponds with those things. Using the right correspondences for a true intention is necessary because it allows you to call in the correct energy and direct it toward your need in a more succinct way. Having a firm understanding of this is what really helps magick be successful.

Spells backfire all the time. There isn't a Witch in this world who hasn't done a spell only to have it fail or end up with a completely opposite result from the one they intended to gain. As we learn to use magick, we are also learning to understand certain types of magick work better for us than others.

One thing that we all have to learn at some point is that magick is going to take the path of least resistance. And to add a caveat, our intentions can't be about a specific thing in a precise location. In other words, casting for the one position as a Harvard professor of architecture is not the intention to send out. The intention should be open but clear. To continue the example, set the intention for a position as a professor of architecture in a university.

When we look at what we want and take the time to incorporate it with all our other needs, we are afforded the opportunity to create magick that works. We aren't met with the resistance of our other desires interfering with our outcomes. Understanding how magick works is key to getting the results we desire.

Often when we see our desires become reality we are able to look at the results and identify why other methods we tried didn't pan out.

JOURNAL PROMPT
Flush Out Your Intention

Before setting an intention, make a list. Identify all the goals you have. Do you need a certain amount of money? Do you have a time frame you need to stay within? Be as specific as you can about all the things it will take to reach the goal you are setting. Then look over the list. What is the theme? Is it a job that affords you time to complete a project? Is it a person who loves you unconditionally? After you find the main goal, break it down into the most concise wording possible.

For example: "I want to be loved unconditionally by a supportive person who shares my goals and way of life and won't smother me."

Next, write out the intention with the least amount of words and as if the goal is already yours.

For example: "I share my life completely with a person who loves me unconditionally."

Now instead of being overly specific, you are remaining open while being clear about what you want. The goal isn't to gain the affection of someone who doesn't have it to give. Instead it is set to bring into your life exactly what you are asking for from wherever it is available—the path of least resistance.

A Magickal Existence

When we seek to constantly learn we are making a commitment to ourselves. We are humans—we are fallible, imperfect, and we make mistakes. To Know is to understand that, and to own the fact that we are not the authority on anything in turn makes our magick greater. Many professional Witches run the risk of letting their ego get in the way of their mission. Upon seeing a little success, they assume that it will lead to more success. As we build ourselves up, we start to forget where we began. To Know is to remember.

Pillars are a structure's strength for a reason. They hold up more than we perceive. Just as our true selves can be hidden under the surface, the Pillars of Witchcraft also have deeper meanings.

In the case of knowing, the idea encompasses much more than we initially imagine.

To Know is to be humble because when we lose our humility we stop learning about ourselves, our magick, our processes, and our personal history. The reason this pillar holds magick up is because it serves as a reminder that no matter how much we do know, it isn't enough. We are never finished learning, never finished understanding ourselves, and we are never going to know all the ways that we can use magick to enhance our lives.

TRY THIS
Open the Road Wisdom Candle Meditation

Road opener spells are exactly what they sound like. They are meant to open the pathway to something. The following is a spell for wisdom that can be used when seeking guidance. It is meant to help you find your way through introspection.

You Will Need
- Lemon peel, for uplifting energy, clarity, and rejuvenation
- Bay leaves, for wisdom
- Red pepper, for empowerment and strength
- Solomon's seal, for wisdom
- Mint, for cleansing and inspiration
- Allspice, for positivity
- Hyssop, for purification and cleansing
- Frankincense, for healing, as a spell booster, intuition, and spiritual connection
- Extra virgin olive oil, to help the ingredients stick to your candles

• Three candles in the following colors:

   – Orange, for intellect

   – Yellow, for learning, wisdom, and logic

   – Blue, for clarity of mind

• If needed, an incense burner and charcoal tablet

The Process

Grind your ingredients as finely as you can. Mix them on a flat surface and stir them with your finger in a clockwise motion while focusing on what you need guidance for. Pour your oil onto a separate flat surface and roll your candles through the oil, then through the herbs. Place the candles into a holder and let them set for a moment.

Collect any leftover herbs and place them in a container.

Find a quiet place where you can spend some time alone. Bring your journal to write in and set up a safe place to burn your candles. Using a charcoal tablet or in a small fire pit, create a place where you can burn the excess herb mixture.

When you are ready, light your candles. Then, in an incense burner or in the fire pit you've created, light your herb mixture. While breathing in the smoke from the herbs begin to meditate for guidance. When thoughts come to you write them down. Focus on your needs. Allow the Source to speak to you through your clair-senses and record everything in your book. Continue to meditate for the guidance you seek until the candles have burned out.

Moving Forward in Knowledge

Whether your knowledge is prevalent like a windstorm or silently existent like the air we breathe, it is there nonetheless. To Know is to have confidence in the wisdom you possess and to have faith that if necessary you can gain more. And yet, this pillar is not about the information learned over time; it is about what you are willing to do in order to learn more. To Know is about what one does with their knowledge rather than simply having it.

What a Witch must do is continue to learn, always. They must be aware that they will never know it all. This is the magick of the pillar. To Know isn't a reference to becoming a know it all but rather an invitation to never stop learning. When we embrace the magick of this pillar we accept the idea that every rock we turn has a lesson, we acknowledge that every stumble we take holds a key to our growth. Knowledge is power, so when Witches seek more power, it is through information that they do so.

I invite you to go out and find all the wisdom you can and in doing so, use it wisely. Discover the secrets of magick with as much gusto as you would uncover the truth of your true desires. Use your knowledge to better the world around you. Manifest change with an understanding that you are a force to be reckoned with. You are like the air; you are imbued with the wisdom of the gods. Hold tight to the understanding you gain in knowing who you are. And go forth into this world to spread the wisdom you learn, because to Know is to teach as well.

Suggested Reading

Llewellyn's Complete Book of Correspondences: A Comprehensive and Cross-Referenced Resource for Pagans and Wiccans by Sandra Kynes. Llewellyn Publications, 2013.

The Witch's Book of Power by Devin Hunter. Llewellyn Publishing, 2016.

11
There Is Magick in Gratitude

While the four pillars hold up the structure of magick, there is another piece to the makeup of a magickal practice. Gratitude is like the roof that sits on the pillars of Witchcraft. It is in giving thanks that all magick is protected from the forces that would stand in the way of manifesting. Taking the time to enumerate the things you have to be thankful for helps to shelter your magick from negativity and doubt. Giving thanks for your ability to Keep Silent helps to justify what you keep to yourself. Showing gratitude for the need to Dare acknowledges that you understand the lessons provided in the trials you must work through. Taking the time to be thankful that because to Will allows you to see your manifestations come to light justifies the use of that will. And to Know that you must be thankful keeps a Witch humble enough to tap into the magick that they use.

While there is a lot to being a Witch, the most important thing is a daily practice of gratitude. If you spoke to anyone successfully practicing magick of any sort, you would learn they include gratitude as part of their practice. A Witch who knows what they are doing spends time giving thanks for all sorts of things. Taking the time every day to list all the things you're grateful for will set a mood. This allows you to start your day with an awareness of all the good things you have. Even if it takes some effort, at the very least you will be raising your vibration.

A lot of people find it hard to carve out time in their busy schedules. We all have so much going on that it can be daunting to literally stop and do anything that might seem unnecessary. Others may have a lot of difficulty finding things to be thankful for. These reasons for avoiding a gratitude practice might seem valid but in truth they are not. You always have time to be thankful, and there is always something happening worth your gratitude. Nothing is off-limits when saying thank you.

There is magick in gratitude and a daily practice of saying thank you is how you tap into it. Giving thanks allows you to open up; it calls more into your life. When you leave an offering to say thank you to a deity, they are more likely to help again. When you acknowledge the Source's influence in your life, you become more aware of it, seeing it more often. And when you take the time to see all the things that you do have, whatever it is you don't have tends to fade into the background.

No one's grading you on how you give thanks; there isn't a right or wrong way to do this. Whether you only leave offerings, thank the Source, or literally count blessings is your choice. Whether you do this throughout the day or first thing in the morning doesn't matter. If you struggle to find things you are grateful for, then struggle until you find something, because at least you'll be trying.

My Story: Thank You, Failure

After I graduated college, I moved to a place I like to call the South Philly Slums. For the first time in my life, I thought that I was in control of what would come next. I had made it from living on the streets to having a bachelor's degree. I knew that I was capable, and I felt empowered by the knowledge that I could pull off such a feat.

Even though I had evidence that I could be more, I went back to doing what I had always done: I served food. Working sucks, and it always has. For a moment, though, serving tables wasn't so bad. I was working in a cool burger bar in the Fishtown area, and it was a blast. We had DJs every weekend and it was a hipster's paradise. We would drink most nights while working and it was pretty much just a party all the time.

While it was probably the best service job I've ever had, I still didn't want to be doing it. I wanted to be writing or painting or anything that would make my heart happy. In desperation, I turned to magick for the first time in at least a decade. I had met a lot of Witches since I was homeless in Dallas, but I had not practiced any magick in all that time. What I wanted was to gain a windfall, to be free of all responsibility and afford the time necessary to put all my efforts into my projects. I was looking for the easy road. I figured I could use magick to win the lottery.

The short story is that I spent three years after college wasting my magickal energy. I invested in trying to win money in a game that has worse odds than being struck by lightning. I was disappointed twice a week when I wasn't the winner. I assumed because I was placing all my will power into this game of chance, I'd be sure to win. There was a different plan in place for me, and winning the lottery was not part of it.

I got fired from the burger joint because that is what happens when I serve food. I mouthed off to a coworker and said things I should not have. This led me to finding a job in an iron studio that was close to using my degree. I was laid off from that job two months after I started, and from there my life began to spiral.

I worried about paying bills but couldn't go back to prostitution with my HIV diagnosis. I wasn't sure what to do, so I started selling drugs. Magick wasn't working for me because I had no idea what I was doing. Coupled with the degradation I was feeling from literally feeding other people's addictions, all my failure began to brew the deepest depression I had felt in years.

I hated my life. I had money issues and was on the verge of losing everything I had worked for. Faced with the fear of being homeless again, I figured death was a much better option.

I found myself giving up again, this time on the bathroom floor with a 1.5 liter bottle of wine and a bunch of Tylenol PM. With every pill swallowed there was a wave of sadness. In every gulp of wine another reason to give up reared its head. I didn't want to die, but I refused to end up on the streets again. As a moment of clarity hit, I reached out and begged for help. One of the people I reached out to called the police and sent them to my house, but before the police had arrived I left and walked to a hospital. I explained what I had taken and how much. The short version of this story is that I ended up in a hospital for three days while they evaluated whether I was truly a threat to myself.

In the meantime, the people I love came together. They showed up for me and eventually one of them decided to take me in. They offered me a room to sleep in and a stable environment from which I could pick myself back up. That's when I realized I had more to be thankful for than not. Other people believed in me even when I was failing to believe in myself.

It didn't take long after being in a new and healthy environment that I began to find my way. I obtained a job and started focusing on the things I did have to be thankful for. I started seeing results immediately when I did this. Instead of focusing on spells, I began listing all the things that were going right for me. I didn't care how much money I was making; I was just thankful that I had a job. This led to a promotion and then a new job offer.

When I stopped worrying about what I didn't have and started focusing on what I did, I gained more. Eventually I got my own place, where I lived alone and within my own means. The more I was thankful for the small things I had, the more larger things found their way to me. This led me to the ability to move to South Carolina to be near my sister, where I could become the family member I wanted to be.

If I Had Known

I was completely unaware at the time that I had anything to be grateful for; all I knew was my own despair. I couldn't see that I had a system of people who cared for me. I didn't know that I had impressed others with the leaps and bounds I had taken to get where I was. All I saw was that I was failing.

If I had known that I had a reason to be thankful in that moment, I would not have chased a bottle of wine with those pills. I would have counted my blessings and known that I could keep going. If I had the information I have now on being thankful, I might have stopped what I was doing. I should have remembered that all my troubles from the past were worked through with positive results. I should have thought of all the things that I could have been proud of.

Being grateful is not about ignoring the issues at hand but rather acknowledging that they exist for a reason. I didn't know that I could find strength in accepting this trial as a stepping stone worth being thankful for. If I knew that I could work my way out of my issues in being thankful for them, I would have found the wherewithal to try harder. By focusing on the good things happening for me I would have had the power to find my way out. I could have been thankful for the house I did have. I should have been grateful for the people who would come to my aid. And I know now that I should have given gratitude for the knowledge that I had worked through tougher situations.

Gratitude as Magick

It might not seem like it's the case, but it is true when people say that everything happens for a reason. Sometimes problems present themselves to humble us. Other times, issues arise simply to teach us that we can handle them. It isn't until we can look at these sorts of things and be appreciative of them that we find the magick in being thankful.

When we look at everything we do possess, it is important to know that our gratitude helps to keep those things in place. If we took for granted even the smallest blessing, we would likely regret not being thankful once they were lost. It is important to see all that we have, even when what we have is very little. The magick in gratitude begins to provide more as we recognize it.

Gratitude is like setting a vibration. The more often we say thank you to the Source, the more in tune we become to that vibration. As our frequency rises with our gratitude, the Source recognizes us more often. This provides more reasons to give thanks. In this way, being thankful is like a magickal beacon that draws more to us.

JOURNAL PROMPT
Identify the Basics

Write out all the basic things you have to be thankful for: water to drink, a bed to sleep in, and food. If you don't have a bed but you sleep on someone's couch, that definitely counts for this exercise. List everything you can think of, from the job you have to the sun in the sky.

TRY THIS
Now Give Thanks

Using the list from the journal prompt, wake up every day and start by giving thanks for those things. Read the list as often as you have to. Do this before you do anything else for the day.

You've Got the Time

First let's acknowledge that giving gratitude is always necessary. Manners aside, saying thank you takes very little effort. To make an excuse such as "I don't have the time" is a cop-out no matter how you justify it. Appreciation is an act of acknowledging a reason to be thankful; it shouldn't be taxing. Therefore this practice isn't meant to be a time-drain.

We should be able to take the time to enumerate the things we are grateful for. There are random moments throughout anyone's day when the opportunity to be grateful presents itself. On the other hand, everything could be lumped into the beginning or the end of the day. My daily practice includes both approaches.

In the morning, I start by giving thanks while I make my bed. I continue doing this while I wash dishes, shave, use the restroom, and even while I shower. Sometimes my practice spills over into my drive to work, and other times I don't even begin until I am on the road. I give thanks for everything I can think of in my life.

Since I work with a specific deity, I like to spend time thanking her for the many ways I see her influence, which I recognize every day. I express gratitude for the path I have walked in life that has led me to all of this. I let her know that I know it was she who led me through the troubles I've experienced. I make sure to acknowledge that I am now aware she was there long before I knew her name.

As I move through my day, random things pop up that are worth being thankful for, too. Having a slow day at work so that I can focus on writing, finding money on the ground, or even just a great interaction with a customer are all moments that deserve my gratitude, and I don't need to stop everything to give it. However, it is safe to say that we all have tiny moments throughout the day when we can stop to take a breath. Maybe you can't list everything you're grateful for in just one of these individual instances, but you can use these moments to think of a few things worth giving thanks for.

Taking the opportunities to give thanks as they come to you may work best. It could be that instead of setting the tone for your day you keep the mood constant all day. A moment here and a second there is a good way to maintain a thankful state of mind.

No matter when it is, finding the time every day to express your gratitude is going to enhance your life. Whether it is the first thing in the morning or right before you go to bed, having a single time to give gratitude is just as effective as spreading it out over the day. Either way you choose to go about it, you're going to find that gratitude will not only level up your vibration but also help to bring great things your way.

TRY THIS
Find the Time

Only you know what your day looks like. Spend a week trying different approaches to giving thanks. Is it easier to be thankful first thing in the morning or at the end of the day? Do you find it easiest to show your gratitude when you are having a rough moment or when things are going your way? Identify the best timing for you and then begin to schedule your gratitude at that time. This is something that you can adapt over time, so don't worry if the practice evolves as you develop.

Be Grateful Even Though

Our wounds give us our talent. In other words, the pain you've gone through is what makes you who you are. This is a huge reason to give thanks for the things you may not feel grateful for initially. I wasted a lot of time bemoaning my situations in life. Being homeless and trading sex for money is belittling. It is difficult even now, with all I know, to look at those moments and express gratitude. But the fact that I can do so has freed me from the degradation I experienced. We all have dark moments like this in our histories. Learning to be grateful *even though* is an opportunity to reclaim the circumstances and own the lessons they taught us.

Imagine you're homeless. In this situation, it is hard to examine your existence and find any reason to give thanks. But this is *exactly* when the magick of gratitude comes in handy. When normally you might want to look at the big picture, in this case it would work out better to view the world in snapshots. Here on the micro scale, there are lots of things to give thanks for.

Maybe someone gave you their spare change or a cup of coffee. Perhaps you got a cigarette from a stranger or a warm bed for the night from a friend. When we stop to recognize the little things, those huge world-shaking issues we face daily fade into the background. I'm not saying your issues aren't ever-present, but the small gestures of the world around you will affect your perspective. Appreciation goes a long way when there isn't much to be thankful for. Holding on to those small things and being overly grateful for them is your best chance of finding something to inspire you forward.

It takes much more effort to recognize the small things we gain than it does to identify what we lack. When we take the time to do this, we are reprogramming our minds. Instead of feeding the energy of our poverty, we begin to lend our power to our prosperity. This shift in our perspective will open us up to new experiences and understandings. Eventually you will start to see that there is plenty to be thankful for. As that happens, more good things will come into your life because you are vibrating on a higher level that begins to draw those things in.

There are other, more common things that we wouldn't think to be grateful for even though we should. A sunny day might seem trivial, but no one walks around preferring a gray, damp one. Coming home to an excited dog might annoy you after a stressful day, but that dog is happy to see you. Doesn't it feel better to be wanted than to be ignored? Things like this can be found everywhere all day. We just have to choose to see them for what they are instead of what they are not. You aren't a lonely single mother; you are a strong woman raising her children alone (who is sometimes lonely).

Our perspective of a situation serves as an unspoken acknowledgment. When you can see your small, run-down apartment for the shelter it provides as opposed to the dilapidated thing you want to escape; you are expressing gratitude through your state of mind. But if you are wasting your time wishing for something better without doing the practical magick needed to better your housing situation, then you're just being ungrateful.

Life happens to all of us. We have ups and downs. You've probably done everything correctly and yet sometimes there is no fruit for you to harvest at the end of your endeavors. These are moments when gratitude is the most important magick you can perform. You get to choose whether or not you are thankful or embittered by your situation. Even I am guilty of making that latter choice. We all slip up. We get into our feelings and then forget where our true power resides. The real power of gratitude is being able to identify reasons to be thankful and recognize when we can choose the other path. The path of gratitude. That is what being grateful *even though* is all about.

Even though you didn't get what you wanted, even though you think you failed, giving thanks for what you did not get is powerful. It says, "Okay, I know there must be a reason for this. I might not see it right now, but I know something better is out there."

Honestly, it took me a decade or more to break the habit of disappointment. I wasted years pushing for something, believing it was mine, and doing all the right work only to fail at achieving my goals.

I wrote most of this book you're reading from a smart phone in a word processing app. When I started it, I didn't have a computer to sit at and write on. I would wake up at three a.m. every day just to carve out a block of time to focus on this project. From three to seven a.m. was my dedicated time allotment, and outside of that, every additional block of writing was a stolen moment.

I never spent energy doing magick to afford a computer. I didn't give energy to my worries about not having the best tools to get the job done. Instead, I gave thanks for the technology that allowed me to write from my phone. I was grateful that I could find the moments in my day to steal away and type out a hundred words.

Instead of wishing for the things I did not have, I was appreciative for things like my smart phone, coffee to help me wake up early, a job to pay my bills, a book deal, and the fact that maybe these words I'm writing are helping others who may have experienced similar challenges in their lives.

Being grateful gets me through the day. It is magick because it pushes me forward without the oppression of wants. It isn't always easy magick, either. There are days even now when I don't feel thankful, when I don't see the point. The struggle is real and some days it is more real than others. But those are the most important times to be thankful.

Expressing gratitude for the simple things enriches life. It keeps a count of all the things that are right. It acknowledges that we see our blessings, and it creates a list for us to look back on when times are tough.

You might not have the best house or the hottest car. Maybe you work third shift or your bank account is always near empty right before payday. Recognizing that at least you have a roof over your head, a car to drive, and a job that gets you from paycheck to paycheck will change your point of view nearly immediately.

JOURNAL PROMPT
What Are Your Struggles?

Write a list of all the hard things in your life. Do you live paycheck to paycheck? Are you lonely? Do you need more of anything? Whatever your biggest struggles are in life, write these down.

TRY THIS
Give Thanks for the Struggle

Spend time each day being thankful that you have the struggles you wrote in the journal prompt. Every day while you are being grateful, allow yourself to show gratitude for those things as well, only when you do this, give it a positive spin. For instance, instead of saying, "I'm grateful that I live paycheck to paycheck," say, "I am grateful that I always make it to the next paycheck." If you are sick, be thankful that you are healing. Whatever it is that you are struggling with has a positive aspect if you examine it close enough. Once you find it, give thanks for that instead.

Say Thanks for Everything

Humility is important in magick. Gratitude shows humility in that it acknowledges that you know you couldn't have obtained your end result on your own. In these moments you are accepting that you don't control everything. You recognize that you need some form of help. Whether that help is from the energy of a plant, the assistance of a deity, or a helping hand from a friend, there are very few things in this world we actually do all on our own.

When we remain humble, we invite further assistance because we aren't under a false pretense of our own greatness. There is an amazing thing that happens when you say thank you to anyone or anything. It inspires more: more help, more love, more energy, more magick.

Every person in the world could benefit from getting more of what they need. Maybe you have money but no love, or maybe you have lots of love in your life but no guidance. Being thankful when you receive what you require helps to set you in tune with the vibration of the things that you need, thus drawing them into you.

When expressing gratitude to others we are aware of how other people contribute to our lives. This is a vital action for the growth of any relationship we might have. More often than not we want to help each other. It causes us to feel good about ourselves while instilling a sense of pride in us for someone else's success. We are naturally wired to default toward the betterment of each other. This is called community.

Giving thanks for everything, whether small, large, good, or bad is important because it shows that you recognize the importance of the gift you've received.

TRY THIS
Thank You, Thank You, Thank You

Spend time being grateful for everything. If you are running late for work, once you get to work just give thanks that you made it. If you only have five dollars in your bank account, say thank you for those five dollars. When it rains, say thank you for the water the plants are receiving. When you turn on a light switch, say thank you for electricity. You can do this with every action you take, small or large.

Your Actions Show Gratitude Too

Taking action to express gratitude is often a good way to make it clear just how grateful you really are. We humans can say anything we want. We can fake all sorts of things with our words. Actions show gratitude too because they show how thankful we are. Actions make it clear that we are genuine in our thanks.

As I write at work I recognize the blessing I receive in getting paid while working on a side project. Aside from acknowledging this benefit, when I stop writing so I can genuinely care for the customer's needs that pull me away from my project, I'm showing appreciation. This is because through my actions I am acknowledging my gratitude. I am giving my undivided attention to my job even though I would rather not deal with a customer's issue, I'd rather focus on writing.

This behavior works in magick too. When magick produces results we can show our gratitude in small actions like leaving offerings.

Deities or the Source are taking action in your life all the time. The gratitude you are expressing in your daily practice may typically be directed toward them. However, there are reasons to go above and beyond a normal expression of thanks. In the real world, this plays out in actions like sending a thank-you card or gift when a person deserves it. For Witches, receiving spiritual gifts such as successful manifestation requires more of a gesture of acknowledgment as well. Offerings and sacrifices serve as our symbolic thank-you card.

Since we are dealing with intangible beings, it is a little harder to make our offering. Knowing our god or goddess helps because having learned about them, we know which kinds of offerings they appreciate.

In Bali you can find what are called *canang sari* left in temples and shrines. Canang sari are daily offerings to the supreme god of Balinese Hinduism. The practice is their way of giving thanks for the peace given to the world. The act of making this offering is a form of self-sacrifice because of the time and effort necessary for the offering's preparation. This act resonates with their deity and ensures the continued peace they want to see in the world.

Some deities are bringing peace to the world or great things into our lives, and others are helping us fight wars or creating chaos for our enemies. All deities want to be honored—they aren't that different from us. Therefore, they are more likely to smile upon us when we do show them how thankful we are. It all works in a cycle, too. Showing them that their presence is a blessing inspires them to be more present with us.

TRY THIS
Thank the Source

If you work with a deity, find out what they like best for offering and leave that for them as a sign of gratitude. If you have no deities, decide what you think would be the best offering to leave out as a way to say thank you.

The Source is connected to everything in existence so if you have house plants, watering them can be an act of offering. Feeding your pets can work for this as well. No matter what your spiritual path is, offering an act of gratitude will help to keep the good things coming so identifying that act is important. Even sweeping your house or cleaning your room could be considered your act of offering.

Suggested Reading
Thanks! How the New Science of Gratitude Can Make You Happier by Robert A. Emmons. Houghton Mifflin Harcourt, 2007.

12
Witchcraft Saved My Life

I was born a tornado person. I left a mess everywhere I went. Not even I knew where I would touch down next. My life was a disaster film sans a big-name actor and high-budget action scenes. Maybe not forever, but definitely right now, I've survived the carnage. I walked through darkness and when I found light, it was a raging fire…so I walked through that as well. Long before I ever realized it, something was there looking out for me.

When I look at the life I have lived, I think a lot about how it all created the person I am today. The shadows that tormented me as a child and the abusers I've known in my life shaped me. I remember the decade I spent homeless and the poverty I knew throughout college with an awareness for how it humbled me. I grew strong because of these things. I often tell people I wouldn't trade my life for anything. There is a reason I have journeyed this path; it was to teach me gratitude.

I am grateful for the hardships I've known, for the pain and the struggle. I am happy to look at my life and see a fighter who never gave up. I'm a Witch who kept trying to find their power

241

and eventually, I did. The trail I walked was crooked. There were mountains to climb and cliffs I fell from, but through it all I stood back up. I had the wherewithal to weather a storm that seemed to have no end.

When you don't have a lot to be thankful for you really have to search yourself and the world around you. Sometimes pulling gratitude out of thin air is the only way to keep marching forward. And that's okay. When I didn't have a home, I did have friends and I was thankful for those friends. Being grateful for my friends often secured a couch to sleep on, even if it was just for a night. Showing my gratitude for the little things helped me identify all the good things I had going for me.

I see the journey I've walked as a blessing for three reasons. It taught me the power of persistence, it taught me that I can manifest anything I set my mind to, and it gave me this book to write.

My Story: Transformative Magick

Moving to South Carolina, I was focused on finding my true self finally. No longer distracted by the city life. This was a place where all the stars in the night sky could be seen and there were no neighbors nearby. The polytheistic pantheon of the Hindu religion called to me. Falling in love with Lakshmi I thought I might finally find my windfall. I created my first altar with a painting I did of the goddess of prosperity.

Slow but steady the transition from serving food to working in an office took place. Eventually I realized my calling once again. I started writing and researching.

Witchcraft did not come back into my life heavy and fast. The realization that divination to win the lottery was not likely allowed me to open up to the broader idea of magick. Instead of practicing I simply studied. Relearning the pantheons I once knew brought about a greater understanding for them. Manifestation and the power of a positive mindset became my primers. Watching what I said and how I worded things kept me from bringing about what I did not want. Instead of saying I was poor and struggling, I'd say I was rich in development.

Meeting Travis changed my life as well. It took meeting his sons one time for me to know that I wanted to be a dad. As our relationship developed, we helped each other. What's more is we accepted each other. He was just as damaged as me, only my damage didn't feed his; it helped to heal it. The same went for me.

Two years after we met, we got married. I felt loved and free of the oppression I had been healing from for so long. For the first time, I knew I was worth something. This is when magick really started coming back into my life. It started slow with listening to mantras and meditations on manifesting. The transition into Witchcraft came in conversations with my sister. I would talk about the things I was working on and she told me that was Witchcraft. It wasn't long before my Witch calling became clear.

The day I bought a book of shadows then took a random drive, when I stopped to pee on the side of the road near the lake, I looked down to find the skull of a goat. I knew this was meant for me. I picked it up and brought it home. Next came the night I wrote my first spell.

I wanted to draw down the moon to call on my power as a Witch once and for all. I decided to contain my magick in a talisman that I could wear around my neck. I designed my ritual and prepared everything to be performed on the three nights surrounding the full moon. Initially I had a plan to call out to three deities, but when it came time to name them, only one name came out—Hekate. I did not know this goddess and yet she was the one I called to. It was as if I was drawn to her and she was telling me, "I am your path forward."

As I went deeper down the rabbit hole of Witchcraft, I learned about my own desires. I was able to cut through the surface and see the truth beneath the goal of finding riches. I didn't want money—I wanted safety. I wanted to find comfort and security. Through learning about my shadow, I grew to understand that my need to perform money magick was fear-based. As I began to develop my intentions, it became clear that stability was my real goal.

I had already spent my life working for everything I had. I possessed empirical evidence that told me I could achieve any mundane goal I set my sights on. And yet because of fear I never worked on writing a book. Because of fear I made excuses about why I needed stacks of money before I could find the success as a writer. I couldn't even see my own successes before I came into my magick as a Witch because I had been giving my power away. Calling my power back to me and stepping into my calling as a Witch helped me become wise.

As I was led by the goddess Hekate I began to learn more about me, to heal in ways I didn't know I needed to. I started leaving offerings on the dark moon and giving gratitude to Hekate each morning. And then the day of the storm came, the day everything from before being a Witch was finally washed away.

I went for a walk in a small town while my husband was checking out a new gym. The sky started as blue but there was an electric charge to the air that stirred around me. I walked as if led by some unknown force eventually ending up at a parking garage. Climbing the stairs, I knew I was being drawn forward. As I reached the top I could see a black wall of a cloud rolling in. This was the Titaness.

The rain began heavy and all around me was lightning. The storm rose as if out of nowhere and it poured, soaking me to my bones. I stood there energized by the charge in the air. I called out to Hekate and asked for protection and the thunder clapped over my head. I asked her, "Is this you?" And the lightning split the clouds open. It was at this moment that I dedicated myself to Hekate. I vowed to always put her first.

What I Know Now

If I had some normal life with no real struggle, this book would be full of nothing relatable. Instead, I got maybe a little more than my share of the struggle. And because I got that heaping portion, I now have a gift I can give to the world, a gift that says, "Hey, you aren't alone out there." I was endeavoring to find myself while attempting to survive in a world that seemed to be against me. It would have helped me to know I wasn't the only one dealing with this sort of stuff.

If I never picked up the tarot or learned to understand the clairsenses; if I never walked away from the god of Abraham or learned to protect myself, I wouldn't be the Witch I am today. If I never learned to Keep Silent, to Dare, to Know, and to Will, I wouldn't be a Witch. If I didn't learn to persist, to keep trying, to put in the work to get what I want, I wouldn't ever understand that I can, in fact, manifest my intentions both mundane and magickal.

I was a broken boy who became a homeless young man. I became the successful adult I am today because of the trauma and trials I went through. Those things informed my understanding that setbacks don't define me. Walking through the hellfire and coming out the other side taught me that I can accomplish anything.

Everything happens in its own time, often for reasons we can't understand. Looking back now, I can see the reason for my path. Because I'm not the only one. The world of Witchcraft is filled with people who never talk about the hard stuff. It's filled with writers who present a world that seems easy to navigate. But that is not the truth. For the majority of us magickal people the world is a hard place and we've turned to magick in order to help us deal.

What I know now is that magick is a tool for dealing with the world we live in. It is something we can use to help us through problems and deliver us the results we are seeking. That said, magick is not a cure-all. I had to learn about putting the work into the magick I was manifesting. I needed to find a way to adapt my life to fit a daily practice into it. It takes time and effort to gain anything, and the skills of Witchcraft are no exception.

The Magick Is in You

Transformative magick can recreate you just as it did me. I didn't practice Witchcraft throughout my life but magick was changing me even before I called my Witch power. We all have access to magick. It is in the air we breathe and the fires we light. Magick resides in the earth we walk upon and the water we swim in. Everywhere you look, there is magick—and that means it is in you too.

Life is a trial that we must all forge a path through. Tapping into the magick that surrounds us is one way to uplift ourselves. We have access to the Source in every breath we take, every thought we have. Seasons change no matter where you live. Even if the change is subtle it is there. That is magick. The ability to change, to develop, to grow.

If you are having a rough time in life, know that you can make a difference. It might seem impossible. You might feel lost or powerless but that is a lie you must not believe. You have the power to change the world you live in. You too can manifest your desires. The practical advice I've given in this book is a starting point. It wasn't long ago that I was in your shoes. But through transformative magick I have developed a plan. The mundane world demands a lot from each and every one of us. It is only through enforcing our power in our daily lives that we can see our way through.

You are magick no matter who you are. You possess in you the keys to change your own life for the better. By forming a daily practice, you can level up and transform the world you live in with that magick.

Creating Your Daily Practice

If you don't currently have a daily practice, don't worry; you aren't kicked out of the club. But maybe you want to know how to have one, or maybe you want to learn how to strengthen the daily practice you already have. Here are a few things that might help. Keep in mind that none of this is set in stone: you can do as much or as little as you want. How you choose to practice is completely up to you. I have six practices that I work on every day. Doing these things works for me. If they don't all work for you, there is nothing wrong with that; the key is to find things that do.

Divination

Daily divination is by no means a requirement for being a Witch. It does, however, help one with their journey. Walking a path of magick requires a lot of understanding. Knowing what to expect or what direction to take is helpful. Guidance may not always be found in a daily divination. Sometimes you can have an off day, or your standard divination practice could just not be on point once in a while. Regardless, taking the time to connect to the Source energy for some sort of direction is always a good practice, even if you pull the Tower and Devil cards.

Intuition

Taking the time to listen to your higher self is an excellent way to connect to the Source. Our intuition is constantly feeding us information. Witch or not, we all experience some sort of intuition daily. When we knowingly tap into that intuition, we actively practice translating it into understandable terms. The more often we do this, the better we get at intuiting.

Gratitude

It is worth repeating that identifying things that you are grateful for helps make you feel great. As a Witch, it is helpful in maintaining a higher vibration, thus protecting you from lower vibrational negativity. Not only is it just really great to count your blessings daily, but it is also important to acknowledge those blessings in order to keep them coming.

Learning

We live in a world of cell phone junkies and video game zombies. This is the zombie apocalypse, and I'm just as guilty as everyone else. Setting time aside every day to learn something has helped my practice grow exponentially. Taking the time to read an article on my phone instead of scrolling through pictures on Instagram is definitely a growth-inducing activity. You'll find your practice is enhanced when you make the choice to put your brain back in your head and learn a little something daily.

Self-Care

How we treat ourselves tells the world how to treat us. Spend time each day loving you. This is not an excuse to go overboard with narcissism (that's not love, it's overindulgence). What I'm saying is that each day you should do something that serves only you, within reason. Put the kids in front of the television and take a bath. Go to the gym and eat healthy. Or stop everything and do nothing at all. Whatever your self-care time looks like for you, do that.

Taking the time each day to recharge could help you strengthen your connection to you. We all deserve to be loved but if we fail to listen to our own needs, how can we expect to manifest our desires?

Devotion

Devotion can be a big scary word, especially for those recovering mainstream religionists out there. This doesn't have to be religious. You can devote yourself to all sorts of things. From writing to drawing, your family to your garden, or your deities to a humanitarian cause. Giving a part of yourself to something you value and that values you back is rewarding. A daily devotional practice of any sort can help us connect to the world outside ourselves. This is important for Witches because when we use magick, we don't just pull from what is inside of us. Having an external connection of any sort reminds us that we are not going at it alone.

A really great way to stay with a daily practice is to break things up throughout your day. Giving gratitude while you drive or reading while you're on the toilet are both examples of multitasking your Witch life in with your mundane tasks. Another great thing that you could do is pair the practices up. Maybe your self-care is learning, or perhaps your gratitude and devotion could be one thing.

However you choose to practice as a Witch is up to you. What matters isn't that you are following a prescribed way of doing things but that you are doing what feels right. You don't have to be thankful if you're not, you don't need to love yourself if you don't. As long as what you are doing feels right then you're doing the right thing.

Time to Level Up

Everyone in the world could improve. Not even the Pope or the Dalai Lama are perfect. We all have the capacity to be even better than we already are. In video games this is called leveling up. When a character levels up they become stronger, more powerful, and they overcome their obstacles with greater ease. As Witches (and simply humans) we have the ability to level up as well. Mundane leveling up might look like finding peace with a childhood trauma or learning to be more kind. For a Witch, leveling up could look the same, and also it could mean learning how to use your intuition and other Witchy skills or gifts.

Most of my practice is about self-improvement. I do a lot of shadow work and soul searching. Don't get me wrong, I won't hesitate to hex a person if it is called for, and I definitely cast spells regularly. But by and large, I spend more time learning and developing my skills and trying to figure out how to be the best me I can be.

Leveling up should be something we try to do all the time. No one is ever finished learning. It would be a static, boring existence to remain the same forever. Witches are dynamic beings. We change with the moon, season, tide, or weather. Each of us is connected to the earth and spirit in our own way. Like a snowflake or a fingerprint, no two Witches are exactly the same. Just because I need to work on a specific problem in my life doesn't mean we all do. The Source will tell us what we need to work on. As we develop and level up, we learn to hear that message more clearly.

Becoming more, growing, and leveling up can be both scary and amazing. Never forget that there is always room to develop. Trees grow until they die, why shouldn't we? As you move through life you will outgrow mentors and lessons. You'll learn what doesn't serve you anymore leads into things that you never thought would serve you. And ultimately, when you pass from this realm to the next, if you did your best to be your best, you'll be leaving the gift of well-learned energy behind for the Witches who may one day walk the same path that you walked.

You, Too, Can Save Yourself

Knowing what I know now has informed more than just the spells I cast or the tarot I read. It has taught me that I always had the power I possess—I just didn't know how to access it and allow it to develop. Everyone is magickal, anyone can be a Witch and magick happens everyday. There is magick in real life situations. The way we handle things may seem mundane but when we approach them with an open, enlightened mind, it is easy to see how the principles of magick apply to everything.

If I had known during all my struggles, that I could have applied the principles of transformative magick to my real life problems, I surely would have figured myself out much sooner. But that is not the way I was meant to learn my lessons. Coming through the journey made me my own hero because at the end of the day, I saved myself and learned how to use magick along the way. And that is my gift to you: you too, can save yourself and learn to use magick along the way. You too, can learn to Keep Silent, to Dare, to Will, and to Know to use transformative magick in your life.

TRY THIS
Calling Your Witch Power

This is the exact spell I preformed when I called my power to me. Adapt it as you see fit.

What You'll Need
- White candles, nine total: three for each night of the full moon
- A talisman, to draw your power into
- Offerings to leave for the Source or deity/s of your choice

The Process
On the night before the full moon, under the cloak of night go outside with three candles. Light each one while thanking the

moon for being your witness. Once all the candles are lit, place them on the ground to form a triangle. Set your talisman in the center of the triangle. The words that follow are what I said; you can and should rewrite this to suit you:

> "Hail Hekate, Mother Goddess, and Queen! Be here
> with me in this hour as I call my Witch's Power."

After saying the phrase, lift your arms up to the moon and imagine yourself cupping its light in your hands. Draw the light of the moon down in your hands and place them over your talisman. Repeat the phrase three times as you hold your hands over the talisman. Feel the energy of the moon move from your hands into your talisman.

Follow the steps two more times, repeating the phase, lifting your arms, drawing down the power of the moon, and then repeating the phrase three more times.

As the candles burn out, sit in meditation and visualize your power being placed in your talisman. When the candles burn out, clean up the remains and leave an offering.

Repeat this spell for the next two nights, which would be the night of the full moon and the night afterward.

Resources

If you or someone you know is struggling with any similar situations mentioned in my story, here are some resources to provide help:

LGBTQ+ Resources

The Ali Forney Center has a list by state that may help homeless LGBTQ+ community members find a way off of the streets. https://www.aliforneycenter.org/get-help/resources-by-state/.

Lambda Legal has a resource list by state that encompasses many of the issues faced by the LGBTQ+ youth of America. https://www.lambdalegal.org/know-your-rights/article/youth-regional-organizations-by-state.

Mental Health and Substance Abuse Resources

SAMHSA is the Substance Abuse and Mental Health Service Administration. They have a hotline to call for individuals and families experiencing substance abuse or mental health issues. 1-800-662-HELP (4357)

The National Suicide Prevention Lifeline is a free and confidential hotline that provides resources for suicide prevention and people in crisis. 1-800-273-8255

Sexual Violence Resources

RAINN is the nation's largest anti-sexual violence organization. They have a 24/7 national hotline that is free and confidential. If you have experienced sexual violence, they are here to help. 1-800-656-HOPE (4673)

To Write to the Author

If you wish to contact the author or would like more information about this book, please write to the author in care of Llewellyn Worldwide Ltd. and we will forward your request. Both the author and publisher appreciate hearing from you and learning of your enjoyment of this book and how it has helped you. Llewellyn Worldwide Ltd. cannot guarantee that every letter written to the author can be answered, but all will be forwarded. Please write to:

Vincent Higginbotham
⁒ Llewellyn Worldwide
2143 Wooddale Drive
Woodbury, MN 55125-2989

Please enclose a self-addressed stamped envelope for reply,
or $1.00 to cover costs. If outside the U.S.A., enclose
an international postal reply coupon.

Many of Llewellyn's authors have websites with additional information and resources. For more information, please visit our website at http://www.llewellyn.com